mothercare

# babies' r[illegible]s

CW01619005

## the ultimate guide to planning and decorating your baby's nursery

**anna ryder richardson**

The publisher takes no responsibility for any injury or loss arising from the procedures or materials described in this book. Materials, tools, skills and work areas vary greatly and are the responsibility of the reader. Follow the manufacturer's instructions and take the appropriate safety precautions.

This book was produced for Mothercare by Quadrille Publishing Limited

EDITORIAL DIRECTOR: Jane O'Shea
CREATIVE DIRECTOR: Mary Evans
DESIGN: Balley Design Associates
PROJECT EDITOR: Hilary Mandleberg
PRODUCTION: Nancy Roberts
PICTURE RESEARCH: Nadine Bazar
PICTURE ASSISTANT: Sarah Airey

CONTRIBUTORS
SPECIAL PHOTOGRAPHS: Chris King
TEXT: Lucinda Ganderton
ILLUSTRATIONS: Bridget Bodoano

First published in 2002 by
Quadrille Publishing Limited
Alhambra House
27–31 Charing Cross Road
London WC2H 0LS

Copyright © Text 2002 Mothercare and Anna Ryder Richardson
Copyright © Design and layout 2002 Quadrille Publishing Ltd

The rights of Mothercare and Anna Ryder Richardson to be identified as the authors of this work have been asserted by them in accordance with the Copyright, Design and Patents Act 1988.

All rights reserved. No part of this book may be reproduced, stored in a retrieval system or transmitted in any form or by any means, electronic, electrostatic, magnetic tape, mechanical, photocopying, recording or otherwise, without the prior permission in writing from the publisher.

British Library Cataloguing-in-Publication Data
A catalogue record for this book is available from the British Library.

ISBN 1 84400 001 X

Printed and bound in Hong Kong

# contents

# young at heart!

I have been making and changing things since I could say the word 'pink'. I remember my first creations fondly – a family of gooseberries made from an old green curtain, and for my decorating debut a trail of bright blue footprints painted up the wall and across the ceiling. I was a hyperactive child and my mother would often hear me reorganising my bedroom at night, shifting round furniture twice my size until I was satisfied – and all before I was ten. As it turned out, it was invaluable experience for my future career!

Long before I was in your living rooms doing makeovers on a budget of £500, I had an interior design shop called 'Squidgy Things', where we were lucky enough to do nothing but design for children. We created fantasy rooms, full of fun handmade furniture, funky floors and walls with movable murals – and of course everything squidgy, from elephant sleeping bags to giant bean bags shaped like strawberries or liquorice allsorts. Two of my personal furniture favourites were a convertible VW beetle toddler bed and a wardrobe like a robot with tumble-dryer outlet arms.

Let's face it, underneath we are all kids trapped in adult bodies, and it's easy to let the conventions and pressures of the twenty-first century get in the way. Children are constantly learning, excited and inspired by everything. Young children have vivid imaginations, they set themselves no limits and are always drawn towards brightness and colour. So why is it that when we grow up we feel we need to move into a duller, more black and white world and deny ourselves the odd dose of fun?

Decorating rooms for our children allows us to look at life through their eyes and recapture our childhood. Imagine the excitement you could have if your toy box was no longer just a mundane container, but had been transformed into a steam train followed by a line of carriages for storing away your playthings.

Having your own ideas and inspiration is like inventing the telephone and, although perhaps nine times out of ten it's not quite so revolutionary, it's just as satisfying. There is a real feeling of achievement when you've changed the look of a room or created something from nothing. It brings on the Cheshire cat of all grins and gives you a warm feeling every time you look at it.

The new nursery is a huge opportunity for you to innovate. It'll be really fun, so get into your painting gear, turn the music up and start to decorise – you really do have a licence to thrill!

# get practical

Waiting for your baby is likely to be one of the most exciting – and one of the busiest – times you've ever had. There are a hundred and one things you'll need to prepare for yourself and for the new member of the family, so this is the time to start planning and be really organised. Designing the nursery is a terrific chance to express your creativity. But it's a good idea to start early while you're still mobile and to get things moving before your bump takes over completely and you're too big and tired to even get up off the sofa. I'm here to guide you through the whole process – and don't forget that all the activity involved in decorating is excellent pre-natal exercise for you!

# planning

Planning your baby's first room in detail is as exciting as it is a necessary part of the great preparations building up to your chubby-cheeked cherub's arrival. Like a military exercise, there are many requirements you'll need to schedule into your arrangements, and the more you can accommodate, the happier everyone will be during operation b.a.b.y. With the practicalities taken care of you can then focus on the yummy bit.

Decorating a nursery is more fun than working on any other room in the house – this is your big chance to unleash your bursting creativity, indulge your fantasies and allow yourself to be small again (something we should all do more often). Start to collect together the visual material that inspires you and use it to make a giant storyboard of ideas or a scrap book. Try to lay your hands on every baby catalogue you can find and look out for shade cards, fabric swatches and samples of floor coverings, then work out how they'll all fit together (I'll tell you how to plan the layout on pages 28–29). Aim to create the ultimate nursery that not only makes you and your baby feel great every time you set foot inside, but that also works on a practical level to make both your lives easier.

The seven rooms featured in this book are not just for the newborn – the designs are long-lived and adaptable, and will see your offspring through the first few years of life. Most of the themes are suitable for girls or boys, but for some of you, the sex of your baby may determine how you wish to decorate the room. No self-respecting boy would really want to sleep in Mary, Mary's flower garden, much preferring the buses, trains and automobiles of the transport room! Not everyone wants to know whether their new arrival is going to be the male or female version, so you may want to wait until after the birth before doing-it-yourself.

Whatever style or theme you opt for in your nursery, a sturdy cot or crib and comfortable chair will always be your top priorities.

## which room?

If you've enough rooms to be able to choose which one will be the nursery, go for the one nearest your own bedroom, for when you need

Children, as well as adults, will be waiting with open arms to greet the new member of their family.

to stumble across the landing in those half-asleep moments. Of course, it helps to be able to hear your baby, although a baby monitor can be the answer here.

Easy access to a water supply is essential. All those bits that need wiping and cleaning – and just as you do one end, the other needs attention, or so it seems! A room near the bathroom is ideal but flat-dwellers could opt for somewhere close to the kitchen (which is where most parents end up spending a lot of their time!). If you already have a washbasin in the spare bedroom, that's an added bonus. It will make life a lot easier if you don't have to go on an expedition and back to get a drop of water for those sticky moments. If you're considering bathing baby in the nursery, this definitely calls for rubber flooring and wipeable surfaces. Things are bound to get splashy, so why not allocate a whole area as a wet corner if you've enough space.

During the first weeks after the birth you might end up feeling as if you spend as much time in the nursery as your baby does, so make sure you like it too!

**how much space?** If you're short of space – and most of us are – babies can easily pop out of the blue (or pink!) and start to take over territorially. However, they are adaptable, small people who don't need a lot of space initially, so even the smallest boxroom could be considered for baby's first room. All you really need to start with is a cot and a chair for night feeds – and it's amazing the storage you can conjure up out of apparently thin air. Remember, small does mean compact and at your fingertips – essential when one hand is permanently occupied with a squirming bundle!

**beat the noise** Once they're off to dream land, they really do sleep like babies – and most babies can slumber through all kinds of revelry. But do think about any persistent noise from your surrounding area – traffic, aircraft or a sports ground – and consider double-glazing and/or thick interlined curtains to cut down on how much you hear. Don't forget it works the other way round too – if the partition walls are thin, your next-door neighbour may not want to share the 24-hour routine of your growing bundle of joy!

**light the way** Plan your blinds and curtains so you can control the level of darkness to help baby get to sleep. Lighting is a whole subject on its own and can be used to set different moods for different times of the day and night. Once you start looking, you'll find there are lots of lamps and lampshades in the shops that are specially designed for children. It's important to make the lighting scheme adaptable: for example, it's useful to have a central overhead light with a dimmer switch as well as a table lamp and a comforting night light which can be kept on after dark – just in case there IS something under the bed!

**doubling up** Twins need not mean twice the problems and double the workload! Yes, there will be two cots, more clothes and two of almost everything else, but with clever use of storage you can fit everything in. It is worth paying extra attention to find the shortest possible paths between changing, dressing and sleeping areas, much as you need to consider the 'working triangle' between the sink, food preparation area and the cooker, when designing a kitchen.

If you already have a toddler you might have to accommodate your latest arrival in the existing nursery, which will mean reshuffling the furniture to make space for another cot. Think about buying matching cot beds to give a co-ordinated look and make sure that the older child still has a clearly marked individual space in the bedroom so he or she will not feel pushed out by the new sibling.

Finally, don't forget your old mates who once made use of your rather lumpy sofabed. The new nursery can still double up as your spare bedroom when they come to stay if you plan extra sleeping arrangements from the start.

**money matters** It's very easy to get carried away designing a dream room for your dream baby, but as with any other room you should always set yourself a realistic budget – and stick to it. Not everything has to be new. Look around the rest of the house and in the attic to find anything that could be revamped and revived.

As with planning a wedding list, a 'baby list' is a good way of sharing the cost with your family and friends. You'll find that many of them are only too eager to buy a gift that is actually useful and necessary – there is a limit to how many teddy bears will be needed in the first weeks of life! You don't have to have a fully stocked nursery to begin with as much of the equipment isn't required during the early months. The cost can be spread over time, and having financial constraints really will inspire you to be constantly creative with your child's space and your budget.

For the ultimate non-slip rug, think about painting a rug design directly onto sanded floorboards. A couple of layers of varnish will protect from scuffs.

# walls and floors

If you think of your baby's room as a gallery in which you're going to showcase your creative ideas, then the floor, ceiling and walls become giant canvases on which to let your imagination fly! We are often braver in our munchkin's room than we are in our own living spaces, so this is the chance for you to discover the power of colour.

## up the wall

Plain walls provide the perfect backdrop for pictures and furnishings but remember they don't all have to be the same. Try one or two walls or sections in another colour or a pattern. Contrasting paint or wallpaper can be used to highlight alcoves or eaves and also parts of the wall itself. An adhesive frieze is a quick way to divide the space horizontally and you can use different colours or wallpapers above and below. Even if you prefer the minimal approach, you can emphasise your crisp white walls by painting the skirting a strong colour.

If hanging paper seems like a major undertaking, you can easily achieve the same look by painting the walls with broad stripes in two toning colours.

Paint is good value, incredibly versatile and gives maximum impact for minimum effort, so why not paint your floors and furniture too? Always use water-based products and prepare the surfaces properly. Allow each coat to dry and protect with varnish where necessary.

Once you've painted your 'canvas', you can start on the 'wall art'. There are no fixed rules, although one huge image painted directly onto the wall can add instant life to a room and a large motif repeated several times often has more impact than a small pattern. Think about murals, favourite characters or giant flowers.

There really couldn't be a better time for you to discover the different textures and colours of paint that are now available. Don't forget that the ceiling is just as important as the walls – try sparkly paint for a 'starlight' look. Staring up from a cot can't be a very interesting pastime, so give baby something that captures their attention. Kites, balloons, buntings or planes can also be hung from the ceiling to fill the void and add interest.

**underfoot** Modern flooring gives you the opportunity to add style and colour to a room, but often it is the last element to be considered. There are many finishes and textures to choose from, such as soft wool carpet or springy rubber, and practicalities will inform your choice. Remember the key words are 'easy-clean' and 'non-slip'.

**carpets** A new carpet is not always sensible when small people are around, as it produces a lot of fluff or loose fibres. But if nothing else will do, choose a short pile and a strong colour (not white!) and get it treated with a stain-resistant finish.

**rubber** Rubber flooring is soft and comfortable, non-slip yet squidgy underfoot and comes in fantastic colours and designs to add instant style to your scheme.

**vinyl** Designers are constantly developing new vinyl products with photographic and three-dimensional effects. Although not cheap, they look amazing, last for ages and are hygienic and easy to keep clean.

**cork tiles** Cork floors are a long-standing favourite for the nursery: they're cost effective and easy to lay, as well as being warm and hugely practical. Bring the look up to date with matte floor paint to transform them into flower-filled fields or a giant games board.

**wood** Whether solid planks or laminate, wood still provides the most versatile flooring and will suit most rooms. Different colour stains or paint can dramatically change the look and feel of wood according to your taste (but remember – polished floors can be dangerous with little people around!).

Despite its pristine appearance, this glossy white-painted floor is very resilient and will stand up well to everyday wear and tear.

**rugs & mats** If you think that all these surfaces may prove a little hard on the eye, if not underfoot, then soften the look with rugs (always with non-slip backing). Look for simple geometric patterns or large motifs to co-ordinate with your main theme – or make your own (rag rugging is very therapeutic when you're hormonal!).

You can jazz up plain curtains by sewing a band of contrasting fabric along the bottom edge and adding tie-backs made from the same material.

# window treatments

No child will ever appreciate pelmets, swags and tails, so when it comes to window treatments for their bedrooms, simplicity is the key word! Whatever you choose to do there are several design factors you'll need to consider when making your plans, but don't forget that the most important thing in the nursery is the ability to create total darkness. Very small babies can't distinguish between night and day, so controlling the amount of light that enters the bedroom is a vital part of establishing and maintaining a sleeping routine. Specially treated blinds or curtains with blackout linings will enable you to shut out the brightest dawn or the sunshine on a summer evening. And if you can't decide between curtains or blinds, a multi-layered combination of the two is versatile and efficient.

The sweet appliqué pockets on this quirky curtain provide extra storage space for baby's tiniest toys. This is an idea that's really simple to copy.

## curtains

Curtains can soften a room and make it look warm and welcoming, and luckily there are many ready-made versions available so you don't have to worry about seam and pleat allowances! Look for simple, plain-coloured panels with tab or pencil-pleat tops that can be hung from wooden poles and – if you're feeling creative – customise with appliqué, ribbon trims or tassels. If you want a bit more privacy in the room, you can always hang a sheer curtain behind the main curtains.

## linings

Old-fashioned blackout lining was a thick, rubberised cloth that wasn't easy to stitch, but the new fabrics are much lighter and allow the air to circulate – especially important in a baby's room. If you're making your curtains, simply use this instead of ordinary cotton lining. If you've bought plain panels, you can still make a blackout lining. Cut a rectangle the same size as the curtain and press under a 2cm allowance all round. Machine-stitch the bottom hem, then pin, tack and sew the other three sides to the curtain. If you have a double-track curtain rail system you can fix the lining to the second row of hooks.

### safety first!

- If the window sill is less than 80cm from floor level replace the panes with reinforced glass or cover them with safety film.
- As soon as your child starts toddling, fit safety catches so windows can't be opened wide enough for a small explorer to climb through.
- Full-length curtains that spill into folds look elegant but can be a tripping hazard: long curtains should finish just short of the floor.

## design checklist

**position and shape of the window** Is it flush with the wall or recessed? Flush sash windows need poles or blinds fitted to the wall above, but for a recessed casement window you could fit a blind close to the frame.

Is it a bow or bay? For a bow you'll need a flexible curtain track to fit around the curve while a bay needs three separate rails or blinds.

Is there a radiator below? Curtains above a radiator should finish at sill length so they don't block the heat.

**insulation from noise or draughts** Interlining – an extra layer stitched between the fabric and lining – gives extra warmth and helps to block sounds from outside.

**curtain fabric** The choice is endless, but ideally for a nursery you should choose a practical, washable mid-weight cotton or linen. Checks or ginghams have a bright, cheerful look for a nursery.

**curtain heading** Again, there are so many options here, but as with everything else in the nursery, less is more. Curtain tapes will create narrow pencil pleats, but simple looped tabs or ribbon ties have a less sophisticated look that suits children's rooms.

**hardware** Do you want to use tracks, poles, rods, rings or hold backs? You'll find a wealth of choice in a good curtain department but I like to make my own holdbacks (especially the balloon ones on page 86) and use them with wooden poles which can be painted in bright colours. Make sure any hardware's well fixed to the wall with rawlplugs.

**blinds** These can be used on their own for a more modern look or with curtains for versatility. Fabric blinds use far less material than curtains, so you could use that really expensive fabric you've been hankering after!

**roman blinds** Combining the minimal look of a blind and the softer look of a curtain, roman blinds are plain panels fitted with narrow rods and cords that can be pulled up to hang in horizontal folds during the day.

**wooden blinds** Although these do need dusting regularly, Venetian or plantation blinds look great in any style room. The position of the slats can be altered to control the amount of light coming in, which is useful in a very sunny room.

**roller blinds** Blackout roller blinds are immensely useful, either on their own or behind decorative sheer curtains. They come in a choice of fabrics, but I prefer to buy a plain one and add my own design by sticking on felt shapes or painting with fabric paint. Apply several coats of paint, as the light will highlight any imperfections.

Animal print medallions give weight and a jungle look to the soft pleats of this Roman blind. A couple of decorations on the windowsill carry on the colour theme.

# a safe environment

Keeping the nursery – as well as the rest of the house – a hazard-free zone as your little bundle grows into an inquisitive toddler is simply a mixture of common sense, safety equipment and supervision.

Take safety factors into account from the start when planning the nursery and reassess them six to nine months later, once your baby starts solo exploration. It's a good idea to enlist the help of a friend or relation with young children of their own to tell you about the potential hazards – toddlers have strong mountaineering instincts, so an open drawer soon becomes a step, and they can always stretch that little bit further than you think when trying to reach up to windows and shelves.

## stage one – babyproofing

Make sure you follow the manufacturer's guidelines carefully when putting together your new nursery furniture. Freestanding wardrobes, shelf units and chests of drawers should always be secured to the wall with brackets so that they can't be pulled over.

**cots** The cot should not be placed near a direct source of heat or cold – a window or radiator – as young babies are unable to regulate their own temperatures. Most models have several positions for the mattress – start off with the highest to prevent straining your back, but as soon as your little monkey starts pulling itself up on the bars, change to the lowest to foil any attempts at escaping. You should only consider using a second-hand cot if it is relatively new (so that it conforms to European safety standards), in good working order and comes complete with instructions. If you do buy, or are given, an old cot, you should always get a new mattress.

**bedding** Babies are very wriggly and can easily tunnel under their bedclothes. To prevent this happening, make sure that the bottom sheet fits snugly and put baby to sleep 'feet to foot' – on his or her back so that those tiny toes are right down at the bottom end and the covers come no higher than chest level.

The amount and type of bedding to use will vary according to the room temperature and baby's age. A combination of sheets and lightweight blankets is versatile, but sleeping bags are good for active babies who insist on kicking off their covers.

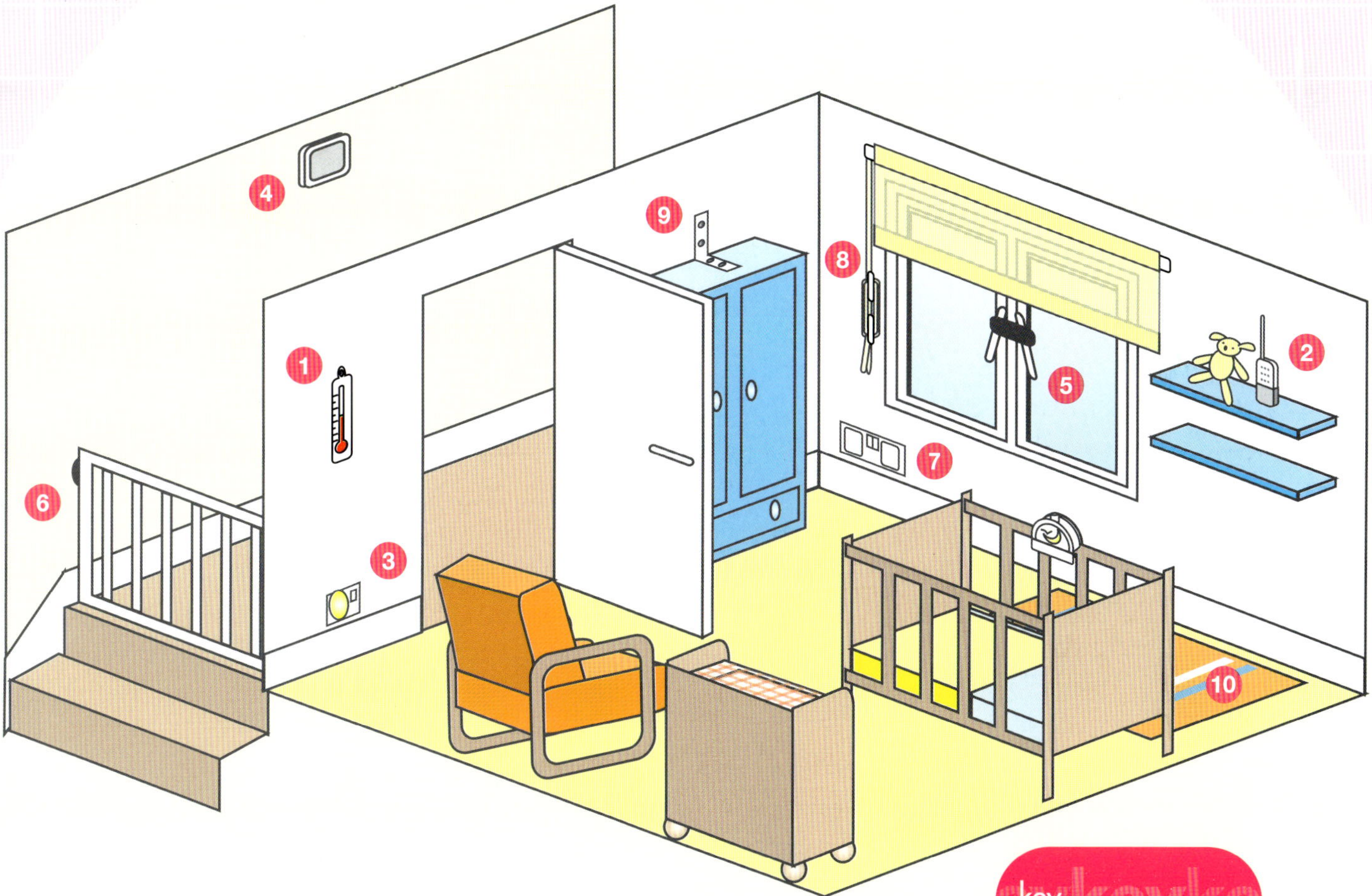

Take a walk around the nursery and check that you have eliminated anything that can be of danger to your new baby and, later, when he or she becomes a toddler.

**key**

1. thermometer
2. baby monitor
3. plug-in light
4. smoke alarm
5. window catches
6. safety gate
7. socket cover
8. blind cords tied up
9. wall brackets
10. non-slip backing

The recommendations below for bedding are based on a baby wearing a nappy, vest and sleepsuit.

| temperature | amount of bedding | tog rating |
|---|---|---|
| 24°C/75°F | sheet only | |
| 21°C/70°F | sheet + 1 layer of blanket or a coverlet | 1–2 tog coverlet |
| 18°C/65°F | sheet + 2 layers of blanket or a sleeping bag | 2–2.5 tog sleeping bag |
| 16°C/60°F | sheet + 3 layers of blanket or a quilt | 4 tog quilt |

Quilts and duvets shouldn't be used for babies below twelve months due to the risk of overheating and suffocation, but in the meantime they can double up as throws, wallhangings or playmats. Pillows should also be avoided for under-ones.

You can use a bumper at the top end of the cot from birth but you should remove it as soon as your baby can sit unaided and pull up onto her hands and knees – at this stage the bumper can suddenly become a useful foot hold for clambering over the rails.

**temperature** A room thermometer will help you monitor just how hot or cold the nursery is: the ideal temperature is 16°–20°C/60°–68°F. Make sure that heaters and radiators are out of reach or safely covered or boxed in.

**baby monitors** Listening devices give you peace of mind while baby sleeps and you're finally getting on with the hundred and one things you still need to do! The base unit stays in the nursery (well out of reach) and you carry your own remote unit around the house, listening out for that first cry. Some types also show the room temperature.

**lighting** Plug-in lights which simply fit into 14 amp sockets are useful for hallways and landings where they'll guide you on your night-time missions to the nursery. Night lights or a main light with a dimmer switch are reassuring, but remember that all switches should be out of baby's reach.

**smoke alarms** These should be fitted throughout the house as a matter of course, but especially outside the nursery. Check the batteries every month.

## stage two – toddler proofing

Once baby starts to crawl, stand and finally walk alone, you'll need to take extra safety precautions. Start by getting down to floor level, look at everything from baby's viewpoint, then list all the possible dangers. A bit of DIY will solve some of them but there are also lots of gadgets to help you: catches for doors and cupboards, corner protectors, glass safety film, video guards and multipurpose locks that can even be used on the loo seat!

**windows** Special catches can be fitted to prevent sash or casement windows being opened wide or shutting on tiny hands, but if you're still uncertain about safety, old-fashioned nursery bars will reassure you.

Make sure curtains and blinds are securely fixed in place. Cut any looped cords and wind the ends up high, so that they don't dangle down.

**safety gates** These are a must, not just for stairs but to barricade off the kitchen, bathroom and garden, all of which can be extremely inviting but hazardous for an unaccompanied toddler.

**electricity** Trailing cables are just asking to be grabbed, so make sure they're positioned well out of reach of small fists. Safety covers should be used at all times to block the plug sockets in any rooms that your toddler might venture into.

**floors** Non-slip surfaces are essential, not just to help first footsteps, but to stop the rest of the family sliding about! Add special safety backing to rugs and mats, then make sure that they are not left where they can be tripped over, especially when you're carrying baby. Take extra care on floor surfaces that may become slippery when wet and make sure that you wipe up any spills or wet footprints immediately.

# furniture

Peek-a-boo! Once your mini mountaineer is big enough to actually clamber right over the cot rails it's time to upgrade to a proper bed.

Nursery furniture comes in all sorts of shapes, sizes and colours, but the most important thing is that it should do its job properly. Practicality is essential for furniture – and it should be sturdily constructed from safe and attractive materials.

## night night, sleep tight

The most important item in baby's bedroom, and your major purchase, has to be the place where they sleep, so this should be considered carefully.

**moses baskets** Your weeny new baby may look a bit lost in the vast expanse of a cot, so many mothers prefer the intimate space of a moses basket for the first weeks. Woven from lightweight rush or wicker and with strong handles, they are perfect for carrying baby with you around the house. You can keep the basket in the nursery or conveniently and reassuringly at your bedside to make night feeds less disruptive.

Patterned, plain and gingham skirts, linings and canopies are available but why not customise them to your own design (very calming in the last weeks of pregnancy) – perhaps appliqué fabric flowers or butterflies to the hood and add ribbon trims to the skirt? The life of the basket is not very long, but it can prove useful afterwards for storing the ironing! A few months down the line your offspring will start to become mobile and may look as if it's been sprouting in a grow-bag. Time to transplant to a bigger container – the cot!

This traditional woven crib on its elegant metal stand is given a contemporary look with drapes in crisp red-and-white gingham.

**cribs** Made from wood and slightly larger than a moses basket, a crib is more expensive to start with but will usually last a little longer. The most useful type is mounted on an adjustable wheeled stand and has one side that can be lowered so baby can sleep alongside you. Bedside cots with one removable side are also available for positioning right next to your bed.

**cots** There is a huge variety of cots and cot beds on the market and countless design options, from the most spartan wooden 'cage' or a fold-away cot that can be stored under a double bed to the most luxurious hand-built sleigh bed. Whatever the theme you've established for the nursery (and the limits of your budget), with a bit of research you'll find something that fits in perfectly.

Most cots are made from pine or harder woods such as beech and rubberwood from sustainable forests and come in natural, painted or colourwashed finishes. All have to meet stringent European safety standards – the bars have to be close enough together to prevent a small head popping through them, and the construction has to be sound. This means that you can't alter the cot structurally, and you should only repaint it with non-toxic paints (although you can buy space-age silver models). You can always add extra decoration – soft items, like a foam name or number plate (see my version of this on page 81) – but anything that is attached to a cot must be either out of reach of chubby fingers or secured properly. And remember that any ties, including those for bumpers, should be no longer than 25cm.

The sides of this cot are cunningly designed to be removed and the bottom end replaced with a foot board once your cherub's ready for a bed.

**cot beds** If you have the space it's worth thinking about a cot bed, which as you would imagine, is a cot that can be adapted as a bed for a toddler. They are larger and will last a lot longer than a cot – up to five years – but if your family expands you may find you need the cot again before your toddler grows out of the bed! The two sides can be removed once baby starts trying to climb over them and the foot board can be shortened (or replaced with the alternative foot board supplied) to make the cot into a scaled-down bed.

**mattresses** These are sold separately and it's well worth spending time doing some proper research into what's on the market. You should always buy a new mattress for a new baby and make sure the one you choose conforms to British Safety standards. For a moses basket you'll need an oval-shaped flat mattress which fits snugly and which has a waterproof cover (very important in those early days!). Crib mattresses are square-ended and a little thicker.

This country-style wooden dresser is a classic piece of furniture that will never appear too babyish for an older child's bedroom.

Cot mattresses have two different fillings: basic foam or interior-sprung natural cotton. Both types are also available with hygienic hypoallergenic, washable, zip-off top layers. The gap between mattress and bars should be no more that 4cm all round to prevent baby's arms or legs getting stuck.

## daytime necessities

The fun doesn't end when you've decided where your babe will sleep. There are a few other items of furniture to think about for the nursery. You might choose them to co-ordinate with the cot or you may go for something completely different. Whatever you choose, there's plenty of scope for unleashing your artistic talent and customising furniture to suit your dream nursery.

### extra cot features

The look of a cot – its styling and finish – is probably what will appeal to you most, but there are a few useful extra features to look out for when making your choice:

**teething rails** These plastic strips protect the side rails when baby's teething and prevent the cot from looking as if it's been gnawed by a beaver!

**drop sides** Most cots have one side (with child-proof catches) which you can lower when laying baby on the mattress. Some need two hands to operate – not ideal when you have a sleepy infant in your arms – so look out for those which can be worked one hand or a with a simple push of the leg.

**variable base positions** Younger and more immobile babies can be put to sleep with their mattress at the highest position to save you bending, then as they get older and start to pull themselves up on the bars, you can lower the base two or more times.

**wheels** Lockable castors are useful if you're going to move the cot around – in the spare room for example – or if you're a very conscientious cleaner!

### changing unit

The changing unit is bound to be the most useful piece of furniture and – as the newly appointed domestic mechanic – the place where you'll find yourself performing all the cleaning-up operations. Its top surface must be solid and large enough to accommodate a padded, waterproof changing mat and it should have three built-up sides to stop baby rolling off. Another warning – you should never turn your back or even blink for very long while changing a nappy! What goes on beneath the changing area is largely up to you. You'll need lots of space for the maintenance equipment, so decide if you want a cupboard, drawers or a combination of the two. Open-shelved dressers are versatile and can really add to the look of the room if you fit them out with customised baskets (see pages 35, 40 and 46) or storage boxes. Extra shelves positioned directly above the unit (but out of babe's ever-growing reach) will give you easy access to creams, powders and all those lovely-smelling bits and pieces.

### wardrobe

A wardrobe isn't necessarily a first purchase, but as babies get bigger, so do their clothes and you'll soon need to hang them up properly.

Purpose-built small wardrobes are soon outgrown but there are plenty of alternatives about that, although not full adult size, will still last until your child is choosing what goes inside. But a wardrobe can be boring. Once you've found what you want, then take a second look and think of it as the basis for a magical transformation. Be creative – why shouldn't it turn into a fantasy house, gothic castle or a sentry box? All you've got to do is to paint the doors and add a few extra design features (see page 37 for ideas) – even the cheapest melamine doors can be painted if treated correctly first.

Off to the seaside! For a room with a nautical theme, try disguising a pair of cupboards as weather-boarded beach huts, complete with porthole windows.

**chest of drawers** Even though we are talking about people a quarter our size, they still have just as many, if not more, clothes, so a set of good deep drawers is a must. Why not buy something adult size (which will last forever) and then add little munchkin-friendly touches like replacing the handles or painting them in bright colours to look like ladybirds – see page 60 – flowers, sweeties or tropical fish. You can always change them into something else as your child ages. And if you're short on space, why not buy a changing unit which is also a chest of drawers?

**chair** As well as somewhere to sit during the day, you will need somewhere comfortable to park your weary behind in the middle of the night, when feeding your little darling yet again! So make sure you have an armchair with comfy cushions and a well-padded back and seat – one that's colourful enough for you to spot in the dark. Generations have nursed their babes on a simple rocking chair, but if you've got the space, you could go the full hog and buy a proper rocker-glider with a matching foot stool.

You don't always have to buy new. Update an old and ungainly wardrobe and give it a fresh, younger look with a simple painted finish.

A toy box holds lots of toys. This one also doubles up as a window seat with the addition of a padded top and a collection of squashy cushions.

# storage

However many cupboards and shelves you plan into your home you'll find that they'll soon fill up with essential items and unessential clutter. If you do find it difficult to throw things away, then at least make sure it can all be stored. With children the volume problem can escalate into gigantic proportions.... toys, equipment, clothes, more toys, more equipment, more clothes!! But don't panic. Storage comes in many disguises, some more obvious than others, so you should find one that will answer your needs.

If you're handy with your woodworking tools, why not custom-build a shelf unit and turn it into a jolly pantechnicon crammed with books and toys?

**furniture** Basic items of furniture have already been covered on pages 18–21, but freestanding chests of drawers, shelves, cupboards and wardrobes are still the quickest way to create storage space in the nursery. Make them even more hard-working with extra devices to maximise the internal space – shoe holders and nappy stackers can be hung from rails or hooks, folding sock dividers break up a large drawer into small manageable units, and extra shelves create more room for piles of tiny folded clothes.

**shelves** Shelving is essential for books and all those toys that are too attractive to put away. It's not only the most obvious storage solution, it is also a practical way to make use of dead wall space. Ready-made units make good bookcases, but you can easily make your own shelves for a more personal look.

Think about making a shelf in the shape of a long caterpillar or an aeroplane complete with propeller and wings for shelves. A plain shelf can be held by unusual brackets, such as butterflies (see page 48), bears, honey pots. Another handy idea is to use shelves to hold storage boxes. Try hanging two deep shelves together, low down on the wall. You can then stand rows of cardboard or wooden boxes on and below the shelves to create a useful drawer unit.

**built-ins** There is normally some part of a room that hasn't been properly utilised and could be turned into extra storage space. The empty areas above the door, alongside the chimney breast

A row of drawstring bags is useful for hiding clutter away as well as providing a cosy home for a favourite soft toy.

or under a staircase can all be converted into cupboards, and if you don't want them to look too obvious, you can camouflage the doors by painting them the same colour as the wall and use hidden-touch catches.

## the place that time forgot

Every room has some hidden corners to be used. Get on your hands and knees and peer under cots, under beds, drawers and tables and you'll see dusty spaces just waiting to be filled. You can buy wheeled storage drawers and containers with fitted lids which can simply be rolled in and out, keeping the contents tidy and out of sight, or you can simply line up a row of colourful storage boxes beneath the cot as on pages 50–55.

The back of the door is another forgotten area – a row of coat hooks here provides instant hanging space for toy and laundry bags. Toy tidies – useful sets of hanging pockets for small items – can be hung from the side of the cot, the door or the wall, and are useful near the changing unit.

If space is really tight you can utilise the area below the changing surface both for hanging a small person's clothes and storing their books.

## controlling the toy menace

Toy boxes are really a subject on their own, as you'll find that toys will just multiply to become your biggest storage nightmare and you will never seem to have enough storage space. Plain boxes or built-in fitted toy boxes are the perfect place to stuff toys away at the end of the day, and you can close the lid and pretend they're not there (until next morning of course!).

But they don't have to just look boring and practical. A simple stencilled name or motif can personalise a plain box or you could transform the box into a car, boat or train by adding cut-out MDF shapes and a few coats of paint (see page 80). You never know – it could encourage your kids to put their toys away as they get older! Toy sacks have been around since Santa Claus and are another clever way of tidying toys away. You can hang them from a colourful peg rail or from customised hooks.

Of course, your toy holders don't have to be specially made for children: think laterally and hunt out roomy containers like funky laundry baskets, office cabinets, old-fashioned trunks and hat or shoe boxes. These can all be commandeered for storage by the toy brigade. You could even take the peg rail theme a stage further by hanging up a row of plastic buckets, brimming with toys. For a little added interest, why not add giant flowers cut from card or foam to turn them into an indoor garden?

# equipment and toys

If babies could choose their own toys most of them would go for the ones that make the most noise! A toy like this helps develop hand-eye co-ordination.

When it comes to equipment, you'll soon realise just how much you need to run one tiny creature. The list seems endless, but remember that some of the paraphernalia is vital, some is optional and some is just for fun. There are certain essential items that you'll need to make your – and baby's – life easier. Start with the basics and talk to other mums to see what they found useful before you start your full-scale retail therapy. Shop for a bit at a time (the high chair and playpen can wait a few months) and don't forget that friends and family will want to welcome the new arrival with their own presents, so you may not have to buy everything yourself.

A dangling collection of Noah's ark animals are a real favourite with the upwardly mobile baby!

**changing babies** Your changing unit is the obvious place to store all the maintenance equipment for the day's regular pit stops! You'll need a padded (and waterproof!) mat to go on top and drawers or baskets to keep nappies, cream, wipes and disposal bags close to hand. A nappy bucket, disposal bin or airtight pedal bin is indispensable and muslin squares are endlessly useful – you'll find dozens of uses for them, from mopping up to protecting your shoulder!

**bath time** Some parents find it easiest to bathe or top and tail their water babies in the nursery during the early weeks. Soapy babies are very slippery and you'll feel more secure if you wash them in a baby bath on top of the changing unit, which will be at an ideal height. If your flooring isn't waterproof, protect it with a plasticised cloth.

**feed time** A night-and-day feeding system saves journeys to the kitchen in the middle of the night. These systems consist of a cooler that will keep a bottle of milk fresh for up to eight hours, and a heater that will warm the milk to the required temperature in a matter of minutes.

**bed time** Classic white is an all-time favourite, but there is now a vibrant palette of colours to choose from when you're selecting cot bedding, so it's easy to match the look you've created for your babe's new room. Plain bedding also offers a blank canvas for you to customise if you want to. Lightweight fleece, cotton or acrylic blankets can be teamed with co-ordinating jersey, flanelette or terry sheets for maximum comfort.

A plug-in night light is a useful safety feature, but you can also get battery-operated cot lights which project dreamy images onto the ceiling and play lullabies or soothing nature sounds. These help to create a calm mood for night feeds. Anything which helps to turn your yelling baby into a sleeping cherub will soon become your favourite bit of equipment! For your peace of mind, a baby and parent unit monitor will reassure you once he or she has drifted off to dreamland.

Activity toys with lots of movable wheels, dials, cogs and buttons will stimulate inquiring young minds and occupy busy little fingers.

## playtime

This is where the real fun begins, as you'll get a chance to explore the world through your baby's eyes – and relive a bit of your own childhood. Playthings can amuse, develop and educate, but above all, they should be enjoyed!

New babies are stimulated by gentle noise, bright colours and geometric patterns, so look for toys that will create a lively environment. For the first few weeks of life, though, they can only distinguish objects that are within a 40cm range and even then only those in contrasting colours. However, you can now buy black and white mobiles to hang over the cot, and cloth books to tuck into the side of a moses basket – you'll find your baby staring fixedly at the geometric designs and simple faces.

As babies grow and begin to develop their motor skills, so the range of toys expands. Jingly pram toys can be strung across a crib or moses basket, just within the grasp of tiny hands. Musical mobiles must be hung out of reach, but cot toys can be fixed to the foot board where they can be kicked or pressed to produce sounds. Playmats and baby nests are specially designed to encourage sensory development and a baby can spend hours lying under a play gym, gently batting the dangling toys.

Big cuddly, fluffy toys are temptingly attractive for adults – and will sit happily on a nursery shelf to welcome baby home – but to start with, soft velour and smooth plastic toys are all babies need. Look for simple, washable toys they can easily grip, use as teethers, rattle, and wave about, and which won't hurt when they bash themselves on the head with them. Older babies love toys they can bang, pull apart, stack and dismantle, and over the coming months and years the toy box will be overflowing with building blocks, activity centres, dolls, teddies, shape sorters and musical instruments.

### nursery checklist

- changing mat
- nappy bin
- baby bath
- bottle warmer
- night light
- baby monitor
- bedding

**for a moses basket you'll need:**

- 2 sheets
- 2 blankets

**for a cot you'll need:**

- 4 fitted cot sheets
- 4 top cot sheets
- 4 cot blankets

# planning the layout

This may not be the most interesting subject in this book, but if you're going to make the most of your space, it's the most important. So let's start off by looking at the new nursery in a different way. You'll need to get to know this room as intimately as you'll eventually know your baby – every nook, every cranny and every secret hiding place (ideal for extra storage!).

**inspiration from on high** Something I often suggest to people planning a room attack is to lie on their back in the middle of the room and just look up at the ceiling. This gives a mirror image of the floor, a blank and uncluttered space just waiting to be filled. Sketch out a rough plan of the shape, then grab a chum and a tape measure. Together you can measure the width and height of every wall in the room and add these on to the floor plan. Draw in the architectural details – windows, doors, fireplaces, alcoves and built-in cupboards – along with the power points, wall lights and radiators. The position of all these elements will dictate where your furniture has to go. Oh – and knocking on the walls isn't just for effect. It tells you which internal walls are solid (hopefully the external walls are!) so you can hang shelves, cupboards or mirrors in the right places.

All this information then needs to be transferred onto graph paper so you end up with a proper scale plan of the room, like the examples I give here. Once you've completed your plan you need to cut out scale examples of the essential nursery furniture that will be going into the room. You could photocopy the outline drawings of the furniture in my room plans, provided the furniture you're planning to use is the same size and you're working to the same scale. And as well as the furniture, you could add any extra items, like pictures, rugs or shelf units, to the same scale.

**first things first** The first thing to position is the cot, which should be kept away from the window (too sunny, cold or draughty) and the radiator (too much direct heat). Now you can shuffle the rest of the furniture around and play house to your heart's content, until you've created a layout you're happy with (this is so much easier than pushing heavy furniture across the floor when you can hardly walk yourself!).

Your scale plan can then be used for reference anywhere, anytime – take it with you when you go shopping – and should help ensure that you don't buy something that won't go through the door once you get it home!

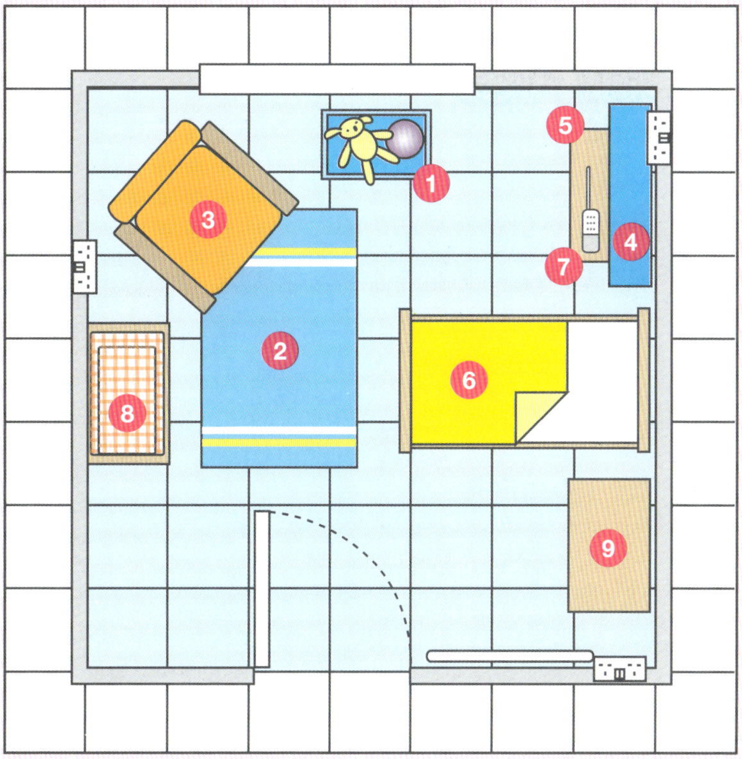

< This baby's lucky. He's got his room all to himself!

**key**

1. toy box
2. rug
3. chair
4. shelf
5. chest of drawers
6. cot
7. baby monitor
8. changing mat
9. table

**1 square = 0.5m**

Here space is short so baby's room has > to double up as a spare bedroom/study.

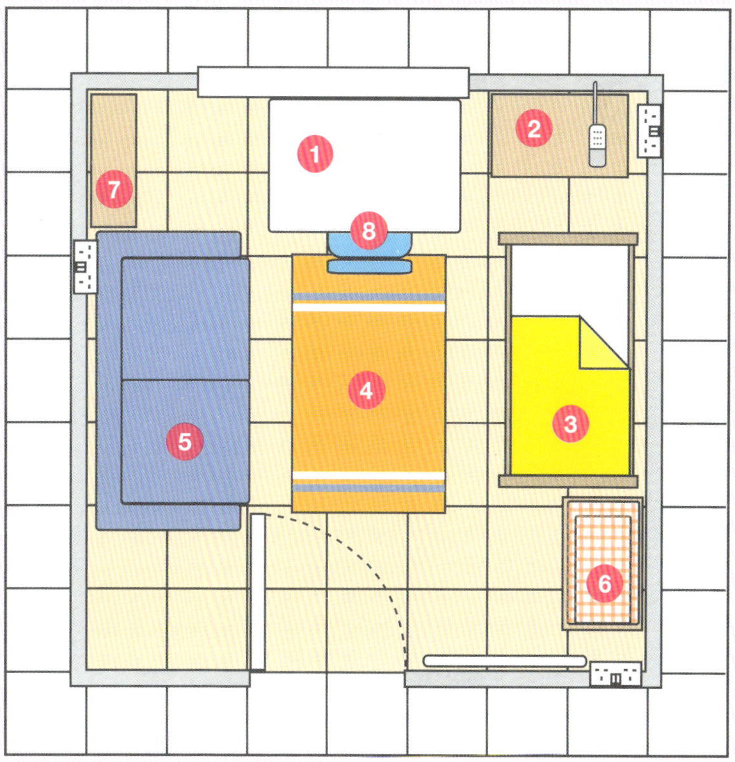

**key**

1. desk
2. chest of drawers
3. cot
4. rug
5. sofa
6. changing mat
7. wardrobe
8. chair

# my dream rooms

Once you start planning you'll find inspiration everywhere. To pull all your ideas together, why not make a mood board to use as your starting point? On the next pages I explain how I designed each room from start to finish, and tell you how to recreate all the projects, giving cross-references to the more detailed instructions at the end of the book. My themes range from farms to Winnie the Pooh, and I've also included a nursery for sharing with a toddler and a multi-purpose room in case you're short on space. There's something here to inspire you, whatever your dreams may be and whatever your budget – no project will break the bank.

# mary, mary, quite contrary...

What are little girls made of? Sugar and spice and all things nice – and pink! As you might have guessed, I couldn't have done this book without indulging myself by using my favourite colour in a big way. Some people are wary of using such a hot colour but if you keep the background neutral and mix in a palette of primaries, it will always look fresh and clean. The floor, furnishings, ceiling and walls in this nursery are therefore white.

'Not practical', I hear you say ... Nonsense! Painted wooden floors only need a quick mop and walls can easily be wiped to remove fingerprints. To prevent the look from becoming too stark, I painted one wall a vibrant blue, added giant painted flowers to another and put a big pink rug on the floor. The ceiling is brought to life with a festive string of bunting and a mobile.

my starting point

## what and why?

Flowers are springing up all over in this magic garden and there's even a small colony of bugs and butterflies to go with them. I think that floral sprigs and flower petals on a small scale can sometimes look a bit twee, but blow them up big and bold and you have the basis for a fun and funky room for a baby girl. As well as blooming along the giant flower border on the wall, they blossom on storage baskets, hang from the ceiling and a few have even found their way in amongst the toys. The tiniest versions brighten up the child-sized coat hangers on the peg rail. And as the finishing touch, I just couldn't resist adding a bright red watering can to water them with!

The main focus is, of course, the pink wardrobe. Imagine how much fun you – and eventually your daughter – will have putting clothes away in a giant doll's house instead of in a big plain cupboard. I customised a simple wardrobe by painting it and adding MDF panels to make the doll's house door, roof and chimney. Three more flowers bloom in craft foam along the base of the doors. If you're brave enough to use a jigsaw, you could even cut out the windows and make curtains that can be opened and closed!

Make this fun mobile to hang over baby's cot by following the simple step-by-step instructions on pages 78 and 79.

To contrast with the wardrobe, I decided to keep the other furniture plain and understated. The cot has a pretty pastel bumper and bedding, but the blank foot board was just asking for some kind of extra decoration, so I chose one of the tiny round flower motifs from the patterned sheet and enlarged it to over twenty times its original size. The three-tiered changing station is painted white with a padded pink changing mat on the top shelf and four roomy baskets on the shelves below to hold linen, toys and all the inevitable clutter that you'll find will just continue to expand and accumulate. These are jazzed up with a coloured trim and – you guessed – yet more flowers!

**flower baskets** These deep woven baskets make ideal storage units, but so that they'll be a bit more individual, I painted the rim and handle surrounds with bright craft paint and glued a contrasting foam flower to the front of each one.

**flower power** This fabulous flower started life as a tiny motif on the cot sheet. To make your own, enlarge your favourite flower design to about 50cm diameter and trace the outline onto the end of the cot. Pencil a large circle around the flower outline. Cut out the various elements from thin craft foam and stick them on with PVA adhesive, following the pencil lines.

## how?

My starting point for the wall painting was the row of flowers that runs along the pretty pink cot bumper. If you've got the confidence you could draw them freehand, but if not, an overhead projector is the easiest way to get your image onto the wall (see page 76 for how to do this). The pink-and-white check curtains break up the expanse of blue on the other wall and carry the colour scheme round the room.

As well as the walls, think about the ceiling. Babies end up spending a lot of time lying in their cots looking upwards, so a busy ceiling gives them lots of visual stimulation and entertainment. For this room I made a constantly moving mobile of flowers and chunky insects using craft foam, which is delicious to cut with scissors and very easy to work with. Mobiles can be hung anywhere in the room, not just over the cot, so you could make more than one and swap them round from time to time. Just make sure they're not in baby's reach.

Baby buntings add instant colour. To make them, cut out long triangles from felt and stitch the top edges onto a long length of tape. If you don't fancy sewing, you can always save time and effort by using fabric glue. Tie the ends securely to screw-eyes fixed into the ceiling – well out of small people's reach.

Baby buntings remind me of summer fetes and sunny days, so should conjure up lots of happy thoughts.

A row of giant painted flowers at different heights is a great way to add some fun to a plain white wall.

Flowers grow everywhere in the magic garden. Some have even popped up among the toys.

step-by-step projects | doll's house wardrobe | flower mobile | pages 77–79

BUS
JACK

# buses, trains and automobiles

The wheels on the bus – and the train, and the car – go round and round! I wanted this playful bedroom for a baby boy to be full of colour and activity, so it's encircled by a busy road with two lanes of traffic, the toy express steams across the floor and a kite bobs overhead, adding to the feeling of constant motion. The bed linen continues the transport theme and there are even two tiny wooden trains built into the head and foot of the cot. The toy box has been disguised as a locomotive with two goods wagons that can be pushed around the room. Vehicles shouldn't be stationery, so even the bus and cars on the road are movable, cunningly attached to the white lines with velcro. There are no traffic jams (or wardens!) in this busy room!

# my starting point

## what and why?

I wanted the cars and trains to be the main source of colour in this room, so I began with a very minimal look, like starting to paint onto a blank sheet of paper. The woodwork and walls are all white and I chose a pale birch laminate floor. This matches the wooden cot, but the other furniture – a dresser and wardrobe – is again white, along with the roller blind and lampshade.

The next stage was to add a wide band of grey paint around the room to make the road. This breaks up the expanse of white and is a fun alternative to a static border. Ordinary curtains would have taken the focus away from the busy walls, so I went for

**time for a change** To make the lining, cut a strip 3cm longer than the perimeter of the basket and twice the basket's depth. Join the short sides then make a 10cm turning along one edge. Cut a rectangle 2cm larger all round than the base of the basket and join to the border, right sides facing. Slip over the basket.

a plain white blackout blind and painted on a crazy rabbit driver. He also stars on the wardrobe and, on a smaller scale, around the lampshade.

The pine toy box – a large, boring but totally necessary piece of equipment – has been transformed into a colourful piece of furniture in its own right with basic woodwork and a lick of bright paint. It's sturdy enough to be climbed over, so all the corners are rounded and there are no protruding screws or other nasties. As your baby acquires more toys you can easily lengthen the train by adding a few more carriages.

**on the road** Using a long ruler and a spirit level, draw two parallel lines around the wall, approximately 110cm from the floor and 40cm apart. Mask off with lo-tack tape and paint the space between them grey. When dry, remove the tape and draw 10cm lines at 15cm intervals along the middle. Cut a 10cm length of self-adhesive velcro for each line, separate the velcro strips and stick the looped sides over the pencil lines.

Enlarge some of the cars and the bus motif from the flat sheet – or use motifs from book illustrations or other fabrics – so that they are in proportion with the road. Cut out the main shapes from thick craft foam and add details – windows, wheels, letters and so on – made of 2mm foam stuck on with PVA adhesive. Finish off by sticking the remaining velcro to the back of the vehicles and parking them on the white lines.

Jack's obviously going to be a car fanatic when he grows up. Make this personalised number plate by following the simple step-by-step instructions on page 81.

Finally, I wanted to bring movement to the ceiling – a kite with a colourful tail does the trick perfectly. It's suspended by almost invisible nylon thread. Fishing wire will do and you get a lot for your money. Be sure to secure it properly and close enough to the ceiling to be well away from little fingers.

## how?

Furniture is less important than the walls and ceiling in this room, so I kept it very understated, adding only the simplest details. The flat sheet has a repeat pattern of cars and clouds: I enlarged my two favourite motifs – the crazy rabbit driver and a cloud – and painted them onto the wardrobe doors. The rabbit also pops up again on the blind and, with other car motifs, on the lampshade – all painted on using fabric paints. The finishing touch for the cot is a personalised number plate cut from craft foam and fixed out of its driver's reach.

A second cot bumper was turned into a matching cushion and a roomy drawstring laundry bag, while more of the blue-and-red check fabric was used to line the storage baskets stacked neatly on the dresser.

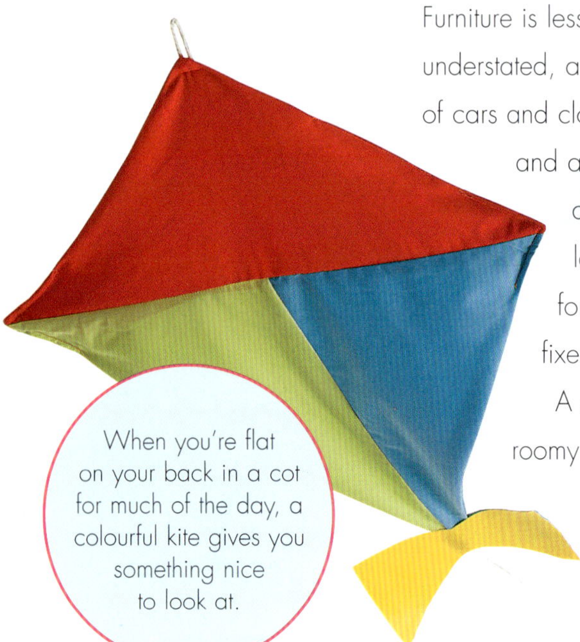

When you're flat on your back in a cot for much of the day, a colourful kite gives you something nice to look at.

Fabric paints to the rescue for a plain white roller blind. That rabbit's popped up again here!

Wardrobe doors are another blank canvas for your artistic skills. Think big with enlarged motifs taken from bedding and a wardrobe just springs to life!

step-by-step projects | train toy box | cot number plate | pages 80–81

© Disney Based on the 'Winnie the Pooh' works. © A.A. Milne and E.H. Shepard.

# classic winnie the pooh

One day Winnie the Pooh, Kanga and Roo, Eeyore and Piglet set out on an outdoor adventure and found themselves … in a prairie-style nursery. But this nursery is, of course, a classic with a cheeky twist and far from the usual folksy room you might expect. My starting point was the hazy colours of a spring day – cloudless blue sky, leaf green, clover and the clotted-cream shades of a field of meadowsweet. But so the look wouldn't be wishy-washy (not great to stare at when you're put back in your cot – again!), I added a geometric wall painted with large checks in stronger shades.

This colour scheme provides the perfect backdrop for a dainty Classic Winnie the Pooh fabric scattered with fluttering dragonflies and butterflies. The butterflies really caught my eye – they are such a versatile shape and so simple to cut out, so eventually they alighted all around the room – on the dresser, as door handles and as hooks. Two have even been caught in flight holding a shelf in mid-air.

# my starting point

© Disney Based on the 'Winnie the Pooh' works. © A.A. Milne and E.H. Shepard.

## what and why?

In this room I've taken the cosy cottage themes of muted colours, gathered curtains, and colour-washed furniture one stage further so they have a much more contemporary look. The floorboards are painted with white floor paint to give a clean, easily maintained finish that complements the pastel duck-egg blue used on three of the walls. The fourth wall is made into a positive feature with chequerboard squares in three dark pastel shades – turquoise, buttercup yellow and lilac – which tie in with the cot bumper, the fleece blanket and the cosy flanelette sheet.

The traditionally designed cot, dresser and panelled wardrobe came in a darkish antique pine finish which I

**frills galore** To customise bought storage baskets like these, cut a long strip of fabric to fit twice round the outside edge of each basket. Join the short ends and hem the top and bottom, then thread ribbon through the top hem. Pull into gathers to fit under the rim of the basket, then tie the ribbon into a bow.

Butterflies alight everywhere in Winnie's countryside. Some help decorate the curtain holdbacks, others have landed on the dresser.

© Disney Based on the 'Winnie the Pooh' works. © A.A. Milne and E.H. Shepard.

**all dressed up** To customise a bought dresser, remove the top drawer and colourwash with buttermilk paint. Cut a piece of cotton, twice the width of the dresser and 7cm deeper than the finished length. Machine stitch a 1cm double hem along the sides and bottom and a 2.5cm hem along the top. Thread the top over a length of dowelling cut to fit exactly above the lower drawers and fix a lilac butterfly at each end.

softened with a wash of buttermilk. This diluted paint allows the grain of the wood to show through and gives a lighter, softer feel than solid colour. The curtain pole is painted to match. Floor-length curtains in Classic Winnie the Pooh print fabric hang from old-fashioned wooden rings and bring a strong green accent to the window. They're teamed with a white cotton sheer to filter the daylight and provide privacy. The ready-made check tie-backs are in co-ordinating colours.

Baskets provide versatile storage for a nursery: they're easy to move about and come in all shapes and sizes. I chose a deep rectangular one with handles for toys and two shallow wicker trays for nappies, muslin squares and all the many lotions and potions that babies require. These sit on the changing unit shelf dressed up in frilly skirts trimmed with ribbon bows.

# how?

The colour-washing I used on the furniture is a simple and understated paint effect. Prepare the wood by sanding lightly to key the surface, then dilute emulsion paint fifty-fifty with water (add less water for a denser colour). Use a wide brush and paint in long strokes following the grain of the wood. The surface can be protected – and made sticky-finger proof – with a matt varnish.

Spray craft paint was used to customise the toy basket. It's much easier to use than ordinary paint and dries very quickly. Build up the colour in several layers, working from all angles to make sure that the weave is completely covered. Be sure to work in a well-ventilated area. The storage trays in the customised dresser didn't need painting, so I simply trimmed them with frills for a country look.

As a finishing touch I sprinkled butterflies around the nursery as wardrobe handles, coat hook and curtain tie-backs. They are all variations on the butterfly shelf motif – simply cut from MDF, sanded and painted. Add metal hooks to make the curtain tie-backs and the pretty coat hook to hang up baby's sleeping bag during the day. The wardrobe handles are made from the same motif mounted on small blocks of wood drilled with two holes. Screw them in place from inside the wardrobe door.

Hanging cherub's dressing gown and storing books and toys here will bring a smile to your face. Make this fun butterfly shelf by following the simple step-by-step instructions on pages 82–83.

**check it out** Start with a plain white wall. Work out how many complete squares will fit the wall (our squares measured 50cm), then divide the wall up with a series of pencil lines using a long ruler and a set square. Stick lo-tack masking tape just inside the lines, then paint the squares in different colours. Peel the tape off carefully when the paint is tacky. You'll find this easier than if you wait until the paint's completely dry.

Dancing Winnie the Pooh characters decorate a lovely duvet cover to wrap your little cherub in.

Pretty Pooh Bear storage doesn't have to be hidden away, but can be left on view to decorate the room.

© Disney Based on the 'Winnie the Pooh' works. © A.A. Milne and E.H. Shepard.

# twentieth-century classics

Not everyone wants a room decorated specifically for a baby – and not all of us have the luxury of a separate bedroom. But never fear. A happy compromise can be reached which gives you a space that's colourful enough for a small person, yet full of contemporary styling for grown-up guests or for use as a work area. A baby's room doesn't have to be crammed full with multiplying bunnies!

For inspiration I looked to the bold colours and geometrics of pop art and twentieth-century design, especially the work of designers such as Ray and Charles Eames, Robin Day and Alvar Aalto. The furniture – the butterfly chair, 'Hang' it all coat rack and stacking chairs – was originally produced in the 1950s and 1960s but it has a timeless quality, so much so that it's still being manufactured fifty years on. Characterised by vivid colour, striking forms and materials that were experimental in their time, these classic pieces have the visual and tactile qualities that will appeal to small and big people alike.

# my starting point

## what and why?

This room has three distinct uses: as well as being a nursery it also doubles up as a spare bedroom and a home study, so it needs furniture and furnishings that will suit all these functions. As with any shared room, space is at a premium and so I found a compact and colourful desk to house all the inevitable office paraphernalia of computer, card index, in-trays and files. The chunky sofa converts into a bed when necessary and is comfortable enough to relax on during the day as well as for feeding baby in the evening.

A plain wooden cot would have been out of place among all the bold colours but a silver one gives a contemporary metallic effect. I made the most of the space below the cot with a row of storage boxes. The chairs – the butterfly chair at the desk and the small-scale stacking chair – are fashionable but practical with their wipe-clean surfaces. And the rubber flooring not only looks fantastic but is so sensible for children. It comes in many colours and textures and feels yummy under your bare toes. I chose orange, which is a bright but sophisticated colour, particularly when paired with white – a combination I also used on the blind.

The walls needed a simple but dramatic treatment to balance the vibrant floor, window and furniture, so I went for giant Smartie spots. I love the simplicity of painting circles of pure colour on a white background. It gives an opportunity to mix colours that you wouldn't usually put together, but when they're popping out of an expanse of white wall, you can get away with anything. Texture also adds interest to these artistic circles – you could use metallic, glitter or even heat-sensitive paint, which will change colour if you touch it.

When it comes to me and carpentry, simple is best. Opposite the spots hang two rows of funky but simple frames, cut from MDF and painted in the same vibrant colours. The clashing acetate inserts reveal a series of Warhol-style prints featuring six versions of your favourite cherub. Repetition is always a winner.

Fill the room with a rising (or setting!) sun. It's easy to do with a simple glued-on circle of felt.

In-your-face orange rubber flooring's practical, fun and oh, so comfy underfoot!

A fifties-style coat rack is the perfect place to hang your little darling's clothes – or your grown-up guest's. It's easy to make if you follow the simple step-by-step instructions on page 85.

## how?

Working with such a strong and varied palette is easy if you follow the simple rule that the colours should all be of equal tonal value. If you just used lots of random colours the effect would be chaotic and confusing – and impossible to live with. So plan carefully and restrict your choice to clean, clear colours. Avoid adding in muddy shades, pastels or any pattern – which would immediately look fussy and bitty.

Visual cohesion also comes from the repetition – the square frames are reflected in the tufted rug, cushion and cube table, and the Smartie spots are echoed by the wall blind and, on a tiny scale, by the coat rack. Only the most minimal of window treatments was needed here: the large circle was simply cut from orange felt and stuck in place with spray adhesive before mounting the blind. I used a blackout blind for sleep-inducing darkness.

The smallest spots of colour come from the coat rack. This is my take on a fifties favourite with squidgy rubber balls (I personally think they look like clowns' noses!) on spindly dowelling – a tribute to the futuristic designs used in the Festival of Britain in 1951.

Funky frames and multiple images of your fave babe bring the Warhol touch to a dual-purpose nursery. Make them by following the simple step-by-step instructions on page 84.

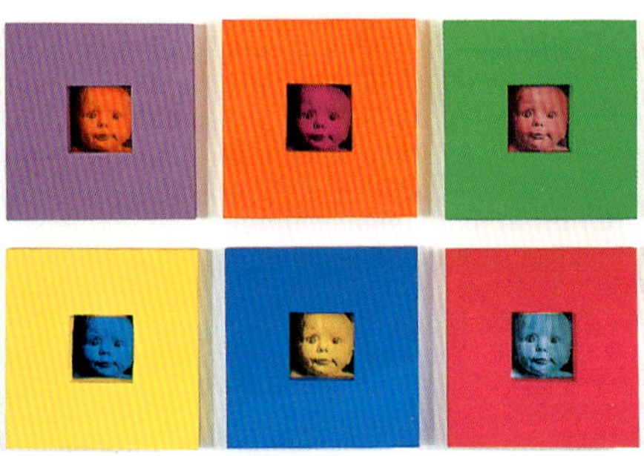

**on the spot** Decide how many 50cm circles will fit onto your wall, then plot their positions making sure that they're evenly spaced. Cut a circle template from thin card and pencil round it to mark each one. If you've a steady hand you'll have no problem painting them in, but if not, cheat by using flexible masking tape which is specially designed to go round curves. Wait until the paint is tacky before peeling away the tape.

Repetition's the name of the game. A colourful rug and a row of storage boxes under the cot are just what you need.

© Disney Based on the 'Winnie the Pooh' works. © A.A. Milne and E.H. Shepard.

# disney winnie the pooh

Generations of children (including me) think of Pooh, Piglet and Eeyore as their first friends, so here's a brand new take on this old favourite. Brought right up to date with a bold, graphic interpretation, this modern Winnie the Pooh theme is not too grown up for a baby, but not too babyish for the toddler who shares the bedroom.

I started with a simple canvas of white walls and stripped pine flooring, and added in a dose of Scandinavian-inspired furniture in pale beech wood, which is almost incidental on the eye. Against this neutral background, I could then introduce vivid pools of colour – on the walls, window and floor – and play games with scale and proportion.

Big is best, and Pooh is a bear who likes to make the maximum impact. A giant Pooh, along with his solemn friend Eeyore, stands guard over sleeping babes in their very own Hundred Acre Wood. Add an extra bit of whizz to the walls with three buzzing bees!

## my starting point

© Disney Based on the 'Winnie the Pooh' works. © A.A. Milne and E.H. Shepard.

## what and why?

Shared rooms need careful planning, and the use of space is of utmost importance. Two young children will each need their own areas for sleeping and storage – mark out territory with rugs and toy boxes but unify the room with matching furniture and bedding. When space is tight, multipurpose furniture comes into its own, although it should be unfussy when there's so much other visual activity. Instead of a chest of drawers, I chose a roomy dresser which doubles up as a changing table for a newborn. As the baby grows, the cot can be converted into a bed to match the toddler's by removing the sides and adding the foot board that comes with the cot.

## how?

White walls give you the chance to make a big impact, with favourite figures (I took the Pooh from the bed linen and the Eyeore from some wall stickers) used on a giant scale. The quickest way to do this is to beg or borrow an overhead projector so that you can paint the image straight onto the wall (see page 76 for instructions on how to do this).

Curtains can sometimes be just an enormous expanse of plain fabric, but they too should be treated as a blank canvas. You can avoid all the measuring, seaming and hemming by buying them ready made. Customising is the fun part – these cobalt blue curtains are embellished with appliqué patches featuring some of Pooh's best things – honey pots, bees, flowers and spotty ladybirds.

Pooh can always use a couple more balloons. He could try grabbing our lovely curtain holdbacks. For how to make them, follow the simple step-by-step instructions on page 86.

Soft landings for crawling babes. Follow the simple step-by-step instructions on page 87 to make my flower playmat.

© Disney Based on the 'Winnie the Pooh' works. © A.A. Milne and E.H. Shepard.

Waking up to the sight of friendly Pooh Bear on the wall is enough to get any baby's day off to a good start.

© Disney Based on the 'Winnie the Pooh' works. © A.A. Milne and E.H. Shepard.

**storybook dreams** Choose the brightest craft felt to decorate a pair of plain curtains. Cut out simple motifs inspired by books, bed linen or wallpaper and stick them onto 20cm squares with fabric glue. Add extra details in contrasting colours and outline the flower shapes with running stitch worked with tapestry wool. Lay the two curtains out flat and arrange the squares in symmetrical rows. Pin and glue the patches down. As a finishing touch, sew a round of running stitch around each one to give a handmade look.

Ladybirds have landed! These adorable handles are a quick and easy way of customising baby's dresser.

When the curtains are closed, they provide all the elements of a bedtime story to be told by the light of a smiling Pooh nightlight. To finish the look, two huge balloons hold the curtains back by day. They seem to hover in mid-air.

The decoration in this room is kept to the walls and floor rather than the furniture. Instead of painting the dresser, I changed the handles for round wooden knobs, which then screamed 'ladybirds', to me, so I just had to paint them red and add black spots!

Crawling about on the floor is hard work for babies, so provide them with a huge squashy playmat. They'll look adorable between the petals of a bright orange flower – and you thought that was just for those lucky fairies!

© Disney Based on the 'Winnie the Pooh' works. © A.A. Milne and E.H. Shepard.

# it's never too early to learn

Education could never be boring in a room like this – your baby boy or girl's very own play school, complete with blackboard – where learning is such fun that they'll never want to come out! It's full of exciting games and toys and creative ideas that will see them through to the toddler years and into early childhood.

Babies are stimulated by geometric shapes and contrasting colours from the moment they are born, though initially they can only see fuzzily in black and white, with pastel shades appearing grey and blurred. Very soon, however, they can interpret the world around them fully, so fire their imagination from the very start by surrounding them with lots of interesting things to look at and play with in the brightest colours you can find.

my starting point

## what and why?

Toys always seem to be painted red, blue, yellow and green or moulded from vivid plastic, so rather than struggle along trying to maintain a minimalist interior, just give in from the outset and go for a room full of exuberant colour. The decor of this room has two themes – primary colours and natural wood. The beech laminate floor calms down the vibrant orange walls, as do the varnished wooden cot and dresser.

You don't, of course, have to paint all the walls the same colour and an expanse of white on one wall, along with the white skirting board, prevents the orange from becoming too overwhelming.

But then again a whole white wall would look a bit too plain, so I turned part of this one into a blackboard where your offspring (and you) can express your creative thoughts. It's a modern take on the old-fashioned blackboard and easel. While you're waiting for your newborn to be able to draw on it, you could

always use it to jot down your baby shopping list.

A variety of traditional toys – an abacus, wooden soldier and policeman and a toy theatre – sit around the room just waiting to be played with, while bricks and chalks are neatly stored away in deep plastic trays.

## how?

When your walls are this bright, you either have to carry on the scheme with your furnishings and go for it with even more colour, or decide on the complete opposite and tone it down, or combine the two approaches. This time, the combination won. I opted for a natural cream

Soft fleece building blocks make constructing a first wall easy. A great big beanie version – numbered like dice – provides squishy seating. Follow the simple step-by-step instructions on page 88 and get building.

A fun puppet theatre in the corner – buy one or make your own – will keep you and your babe amused for hours.

**make your mark** To make a blackboard like this one, simply mark out the area you want directly onto the wall and paint with two or more coats of special blackboard paint. For an authentic school-room look, I finished my board off with a timber frame, varnished and fixed in place with screws and rawlplugs.

**curtain call** This is a quirky way to customise a pair of plain curtains. I found a fabric with a raised geometric weave and added tufty tassels in staggered rows. To make each tuft I cut three 20cm lengths of bright tapestry wool (you could use odds and ends of knitting yarn) and threaded them through using a large-eyed needle. Then I finished them off by knotting the ends tightly enough to stop wee fingers unravelling them. I used a similar technique for the cushion, but this time I just sewed the wool through the fabric at equal intervals.

**hopalong** Paint ten cork tiles in red, orange, yellow and green, then paint on numbers from one to ten in blue. Stick non-slip rug backing to the reverse of each tile to make them safe when hopped upon.

**don't get cross** You'll need nine cork tiles to make this game – five painted red and four blue. Glue strips of non-slip backing to the reverse so that they won't skid across the floor. Cut out the five large crosses and five noughts, from craft foam.

calico fabric for the curtains and then added knotted tufts of wool to give it colour and texture. These are so tactile that you just want to stroke them, and in fact this look started to take over, so a neighbouring cushion sprouted more tufty bits and a multi-coloured pompom at each corner!

The bean-bag building blocks are a soft and squashy take on traditional wooden blocks. These come in two sizes – one big enough to sit on, and the others small enough for a small hand to hold – and let go of course! Make them in the softest fleece for baby comfort.

When it comes to games, you can't really improve on the old playground favourites: hopscotch and noughts and crosses have delighted generations, so I completed the room with giant movable versions made from painted cork tiles.

ABC

# down on the farm

Bold checks say both cowboy and farm to me so, with colourful ginghams as a starting point, I added a chunk of the Wild West to a country farmyard – and came up with a real doh-si-doh of a nursery. This is a room that will easily develop with your child. The look is friendly and cosy, but not too babyish as there's lots going on to entertain a growing toddler – as well as the parent who's just a child at heart.

I wanted a dramatic focus to pull the whole room together – and the concept of a giant storyboard occupying almost an entire wall appeals to children and adults alike (or is that just me?). So I came up with this textured mural – complete with detachable farm animals, fruit trees and picket fence cut from bright craft felt. The shapes can be moved around the green field for hours to make a backdrop for countless tales of the ranch.

my starting point

## what and why?

For a look that's country AND western I went for frontier-style furniture, combined with check soft furnishings – curtains, patchwork-effect check lantern, cushions and changing mat. Once again the walls are plain white, which increases the feeling of space in the room and acts as a foil for the primary colours. All this activity is grounded with a floor made of old pine floorboards, clearly outlined with orange skirting – a good way to bring colour into a room without having to go to the trouble of painting the walls.

The cot, dresser and chairs all have a warm antique pine finish and to complement this I used lots of yellow in the room. It's a bright, sunshine colour which goes well with natural wood and always looks cheerful. I chose it for the full-length gingham curtains (hanging from a toning orange pole to echo the skirting), the appliqué cushion, the fringed throw and the wild and woolly sheep rug. The rest of the hot and spicy colour comes from the bedding, the shelves and stools, and of course the farmyard mural.

No cowboy would be complete without a horse, and when you're too wee for a hobby horse, then a rocking chair will do just fine. There are still more Wild-West touches: a bright red coat rack comes with its own stetsons so you can hang up your hat with your dungarees, and the poncho-inspired throw makes a hip fashion accessory to wrap around your own babe, papoose-style.

## how?

Lots of different colours in a room can end up looking busy and confusing, so I restricted the paintwork to white with just three other colours – orange for the curtain pole and skirting, and blue and red for the shelves, milking stools and

**farmyard friends** Paint a wide blue border onto the wall, then cover a plywood sheet with green felt and screw it in position with rawlplugs. Enlarge the sheep from the sheep rug project to the size you want and add other animals of your choice – ours came from a wallpaper frieze. Copy my fence, trees and sun, and cut them all out from coloured felt. Stick on details with PVA, then fix hooked lengths of self-adhesive velcro to the wrong sides and attach the shapes to the background.

Big fat pompoms will bounce around and make you smile when you open and close the curtains.

**hats off to babies** Cut a stetson silhouette from craft foam and add a length of bobble trim or a foam star and piece of ribbon. Glue an offcut of timber batten behind the hat, then glue this to the hanger so the hat stands proud and there's room to hang baby's clothes.

**ride 'em cowboy** To turn an ordinary rocking chair into a rocking-horse chair, cut two simple horse's heads from 12mm MDF, paint them on both sides and screw them securely to the arms and back. Finish off with a felt mane and eyelashes, nostrils, ears and bridles made from craft foam, glued in place with PVA. Finally, screw a felt tail to the back of the chair.

peg rail. The green felt panel is the only other pool of colour. Coat hangers are decorated with craft foam embellished with bobble fringing and sheriff's stars.

There are still more bobbles around the squashy cushion on the rocking chair and stitched onto the yellow throw on the rocking-horse chair. Here I added lengths of gingham ribbon, but this project would be a good way to use up any remnants of trimming you may have. To add a fringe to a plain throw, trim away the hem from one edge and use dressmaking shears to make a series of parallel cuts along the fabric, about 15cm deep and 3cm apart. Then pin and tack your ribbon, braid or bobble fringing along the bottom and machine down.

Left-over wool is perfect for making the big pompoms (remember making your first pompom?), which add highlights of clashing colour to the curtain pole. The curtains, the fabric lantern and appliqué cushion are all ready made.

A big squashy cushion means you've got somewhere comfy to sit when you're feeding baby.

Baby will love to cuddle up to our friendly woolly sheep. Follow the simple step-by-step instructions on page 89 to make a sheep rug like this one.

page 89

COSMIC
PINK POWER
CYBER

# over to you

After all the planning and ideas of the previous pages, this is the practical bit of the book where I take you step-by-step through how to make the most complicated projects and show you how to turn them into reality. Each project has clear and easy-to-follow diagrams and detailed instructions, and some of them have special templates for accuracy. But don't worry – none of them are difficult, and simple craft skills plus easily obtainable materials are all you'll need to make your own works of art. Read the safety precautions first, then get creating. When your very special bundle of joy arrives, you'll have yet another creation you can be proud of!

# practicalities

You'll need only the most basic woodworking and sewing techniques to make any of the projects in this book. All the 'ingredients' are listed, along with the necessary tools or equipment, but there are also a few essentials you'll need to get together before you start to sew or stitch:

## THE TOOL KIT

- work bench with clamp
- jigsaw
- drill
- wood filler
- wood glue
- screwdriver
- sandpaper
- selection of paint brushes
- pencil and long ruler

## THE SEWING KIT

- sewing machine
- cutting out scissors
- embroidery scissors
- selection of needles
- dressmaker's pins
- tacking thread
- tape measure
- chalk pencil

**enlarging the templates** All the templates are given at a reduced scale and can easily be enlarged on a photocopier. For the bigger projects, draw a rectangle, roughly equal to the finished size of the project, onto a large sheet of paper. Divide it into the same number of squares as there are on the template grid, then copy the part of outline within each small square onto the corresponding large square on the paper. Finally, cut out your paper shape.

**using an overhead projector** To transfer an image to a wall, trace the design onto acetate with a fine waterproof pen and project it at the size you want directly onto the wall. Carefully draw round the outline with pencil, then paint in each area with acrylic paints. A spray of matt varnish over the finished mural will protect it from sticky fingers and scribbles.

**safety first!** Make sure you use only formaldehyde-free MDF and always wear a mask when cutting or sanding it. Ideally spray adhesive should only be used outdoors or in a well-ventilated area with the surrounding surfaces protected by newspaper.

When gluing anything that will be in baby's reach, make sure the edges are well stuck down so small fingers can't pull it off.

# doll's house wardrobe

pages 32–37

## mary, mary, quite contrary...

**YOU WILL NEED:**

- wardrobe
- piece of 2mm MDF
- paint
- short screws
- 20cm squares of craft foam in various colours, plus scraps
- PVA adhesive
- touch-close catches
- wall fixers
- tool kit

2

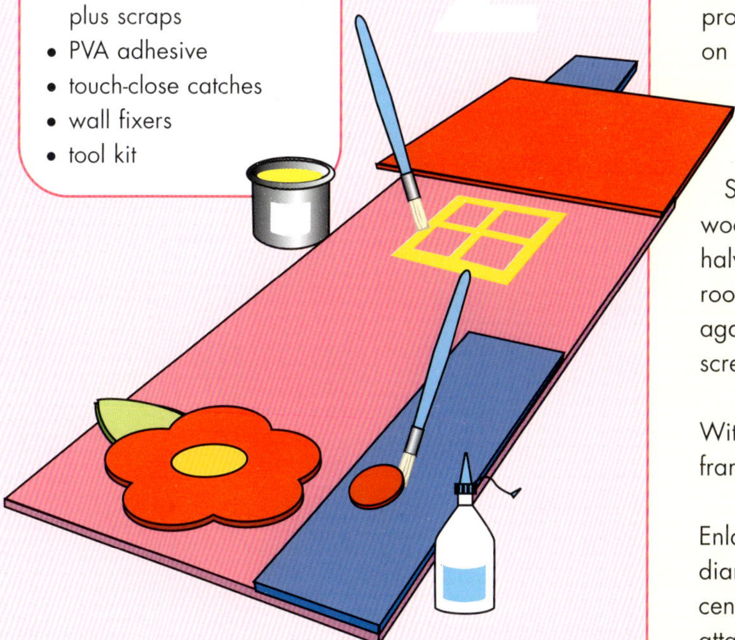

Remove the wardrobe doors, prime if necessary, and paint. If your wardrobe doesn't have flat doors, cut 2mm MDF to fit over them. You may have to change the hinges because of the extra weight this creates.

Following the templates on page 90, adjusting the proportions to fit your wardrobe and drawing them up on squared paper, cut out the chimney, the two halves of the front door and the roof from MDF. Sand the pieces, then paint the fronts and edges. ❶

Stick the chimney to the back of a roof section with wood glue, overlapping it to keep it rigid. Fix the two halves of the door with glue and screws and attach the roof to the front of the wardrobe doors in the same way, again allowing an overlap for rigidity. Conceal the screw heads with filler, sand and retouch the paint.

With the template as a guide, draw on the window frames using a ruler and pencil, then paint them in. ❷

Enlarge the flower template on page 91 to 20cm diameter and following this pattern, cut three flowers, centres and a leaf from the coloured foam. Using PVA, attach the centres and leaves, then stick the flowers either side of the front door. Cut out a foam circle to make a decorative door knob and glue in place.

Re-attach the doors and add touch-close catches. For extra safety use wall fixers to make sure that the wardrobe can't topple over.

1

## flower mobile

**mary, mary, quite contrary...**

pages 32–37

**YOU WILL NEED:**

- tracing paper and pencil
- craft foam
- fine waterproof felt pen
- craft scissors
- PVA adhesive
- 2 x 30cm lengths of narrow wood strip
- small drill bit
- fine nylon thread
- large-eyed needle
- screw eye

All the motifs are the same on both sides.

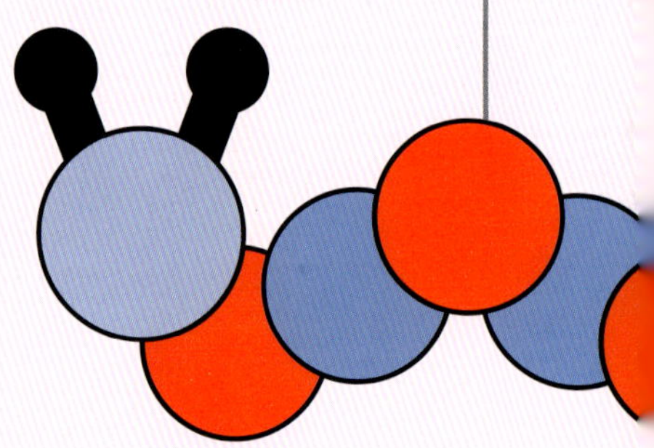

To make the two flowers, trace off the petal outline, flower centre and leaf from the template on page 91. Cut out the shapes and draw round them onto foam then cut out to make two flowers each in two colours, four centres and two leaves. Glue the centres onto the petals, then stick the two sides of each flower together, sandwiching the leaves between them. ❶

Cut out one butterfly and two bodies. Glue a body to each side of the butterfly.

For the ladybird, cut one body, two antennae and two heads, plus eight spots. Glue the antennae to the body, then stick four spots and a head to each side. ❷

Cut six 5cm circles and two 6cm circles from craft foam for the caterpillar. Arrange the small circles in a wavy line, alternating the colours, and glue together. Cut two antennae from the ladybird template and glue them to one of the large circles. Stick this onto the body and fix the remaining circle to the other side. ❸

Drill a fine hole at the end of each piece of wood. Glue the two together to form a cross then, when dry, drill a hole through the centre.

Sew one end of a length of nylon to the centre top of the first motif, then secure. Thread the other end through one of the holes in the wooden cross and tie a knot. Attach the other motifs in the same way, varying the lengths of nylon so they will hang at different levels. Fix another length of thread through the centre of the cross and secure all the knots with blobs of glue.

Screw a cup hook into the ceiling (well out of the reach of your babe!) and hang the mobile from the hook. ❹

# train toy box

buses, trains and automobiles

pages 38–43

**YOU WILL NEED:**

- wooden toy box
- piece of 12mm MDF
- paint
- screws
- PVA adhesive
- 2 wooden boxes
- 8 lockable castors
- 2 x 15cm circles of yellow craft foam
- tool kit

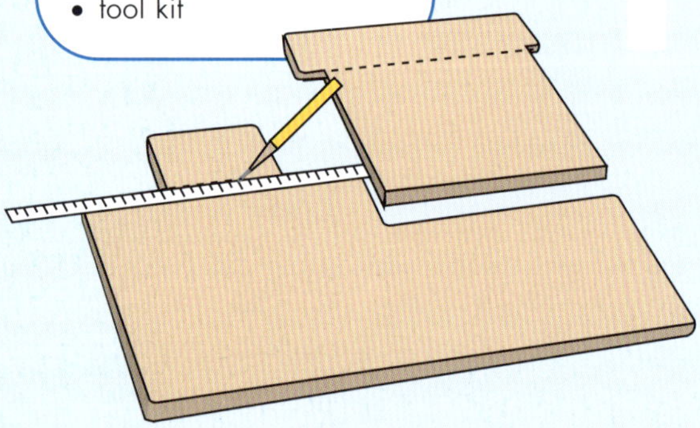

Scale up the train and wheel templates on page 92, adapting them to fit the proportions of your toy box and drawing them up on squared paper. Cut out two trains (in two parts) and four wheels from MDF and sand any sharp corners away.

Sand the toy box, then paint the lid, rim, inside and short sides with two coats of paint. Mark the dividing line on both parts of the two trains, making sure that you have a right and left side ❶, and paint them. ❷

Turn over and paint all the areas that will show on the wrong side. Paint the wheels and glue and screw them in place, then fix the two parts of the train panels to either side of the box. Fill in and sand the holes, then re-touch with matching paint. Stick the circles of foam to the front of the box with PVA. ❸

Sand and paint the two wooden boxes. Attach four casters to the bottom of each.

## cot number plate

buses, trains and automobiles pages 38–43

**YOU WILL NEED:**

- thick yellow craft foam
- thin black craft foam
- pencil and paper
- white crayon
- scissors
- PVA adhesive

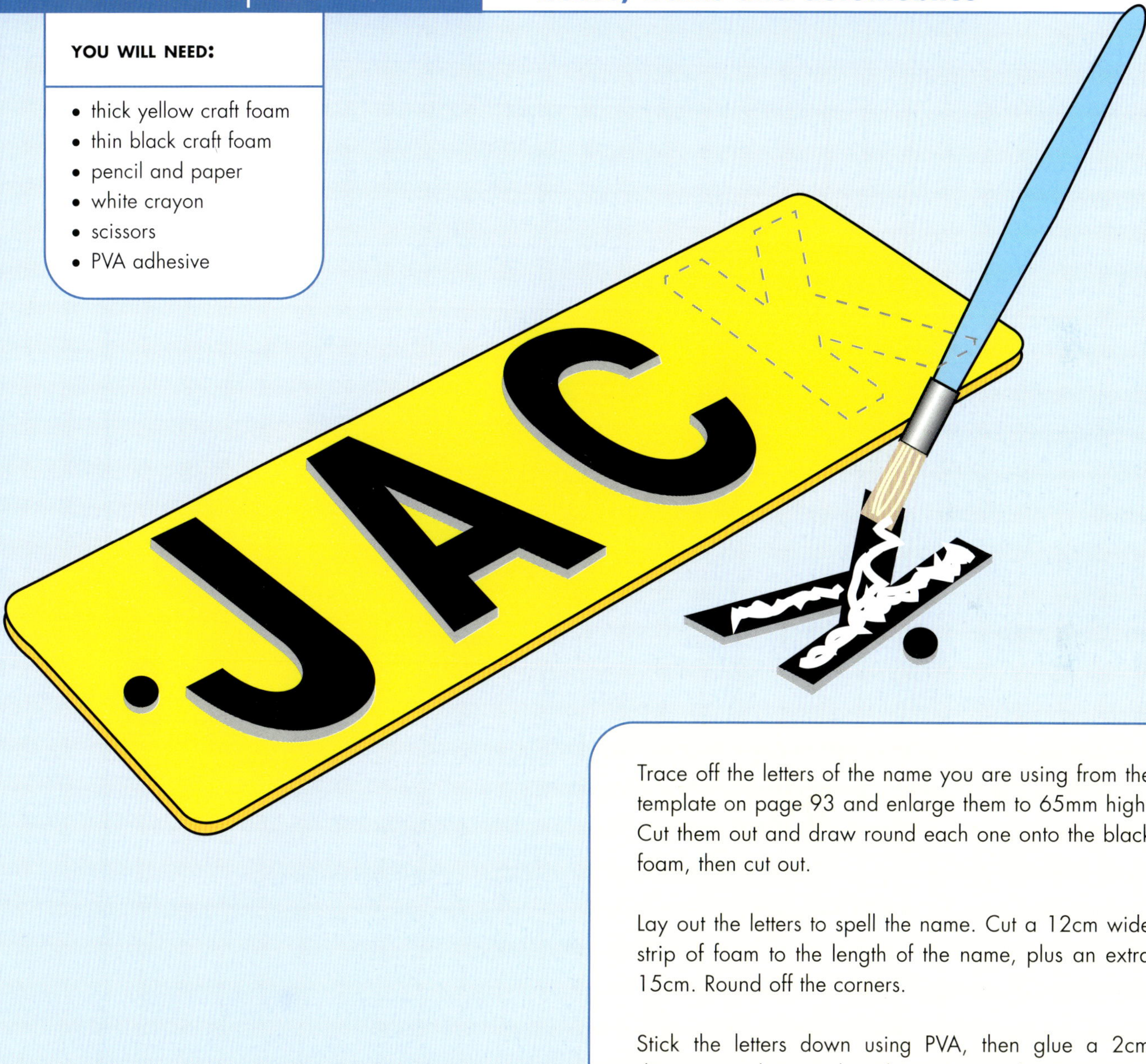


Trace off the letters of the name you are using from the template on page 93 and enlarge them to 65mm high. Cut them out and draw round each one onto the black foam, then cut out.

Lay out the letters to spell the name. Cut a 12cm wide strip of foam to the length of the name, plus an extra 15cm. Round off the corners.

Stick the letters down using PVA, then glue a 2cm diameter circle to each end to represent the screws.

Glue the number plate securely to the bottom end of the cot, well out of the reach of small fingers!

# butterfly shelf



pages 44–49

**YOU WILL NEED:**

- 50 x 60cm piece of 12mm MDF
- 5 screws
- lilac paint
- 3 coat hooks with screws
- rawlplugs
- tool kit

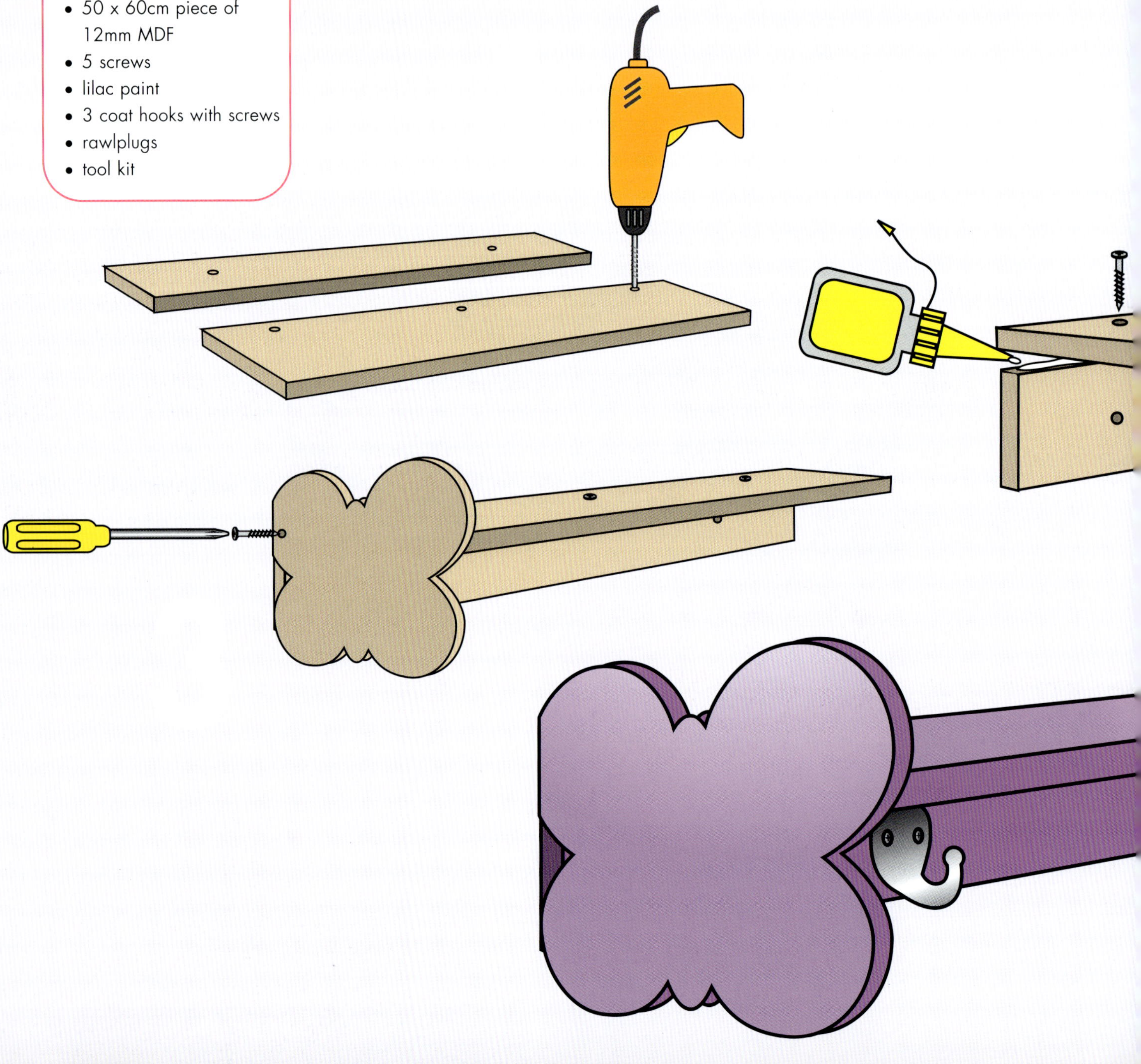

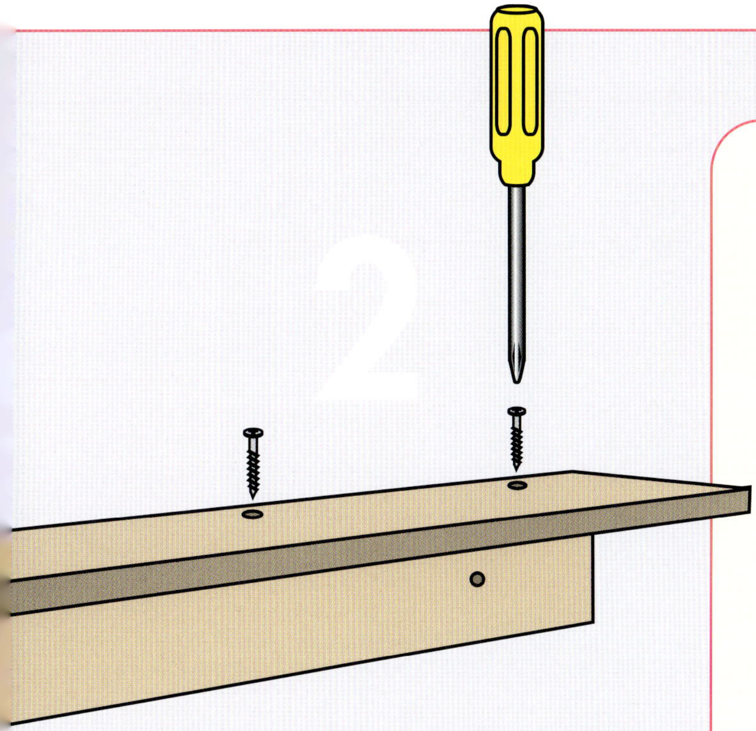

Cut two 60cm lengths of MDF, one 16cm wide and the other 10cm wide. Sand the edges lightly. Drill two holes in the centre of the narrower piece, ready for screwing the shelf onto the wall. Drill three holes at regular intervals along one long side of the other piece, 6mm in from the edge. ❶

Coat the two edges to be joined with wood glue and leave until tacky. Screw together at right angles. ❷

Enlarge the butterfly motif on page 91 to 21cm wide and cut out, trimming the wing along the dotted line as marked. Draw round the template twice onto the remaining MDF and cut out with a jigsaw. Drill a hole in each shape where indicated and sand any rough edges.

Glue and screw the butterflies to the ends of the shelf and leave to dry. Disguise the screw holes with wood filler, then sand. ❸

Paint the finished shelf, then screw the three coat hooks in place. ❹ Fix to the wall with screws and rawlplugs. Fill and paint over the screw heads.

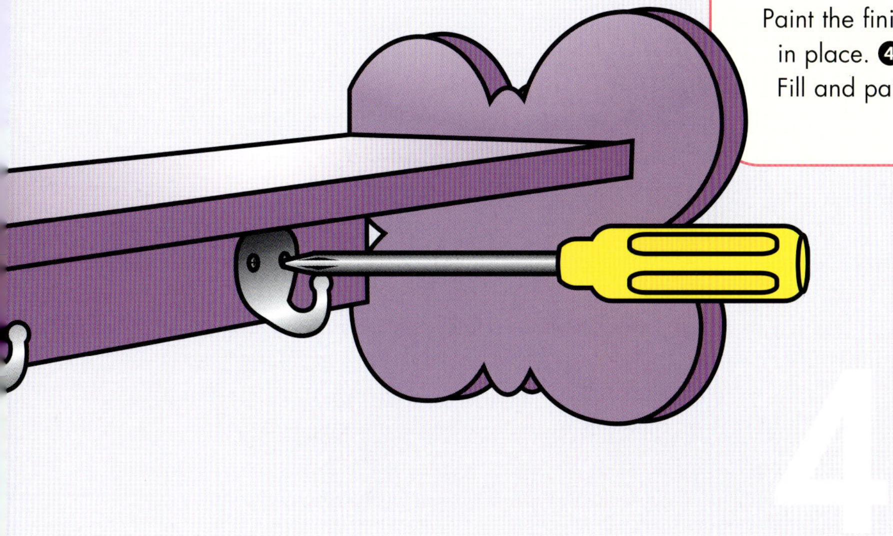

# warhol-style pictures

## twentieth-century classics

pages 50–55

**FOR EACH PICTURE YOU WILL NEED:**

- baby photo
- 22cm square of cardboard
- spray adhesive
- 60cm square of 12mm MDF
- 25cm square of coloured acetate
- paint
- masking tape
- 2 screw eyes
- picture wire
- tool kit

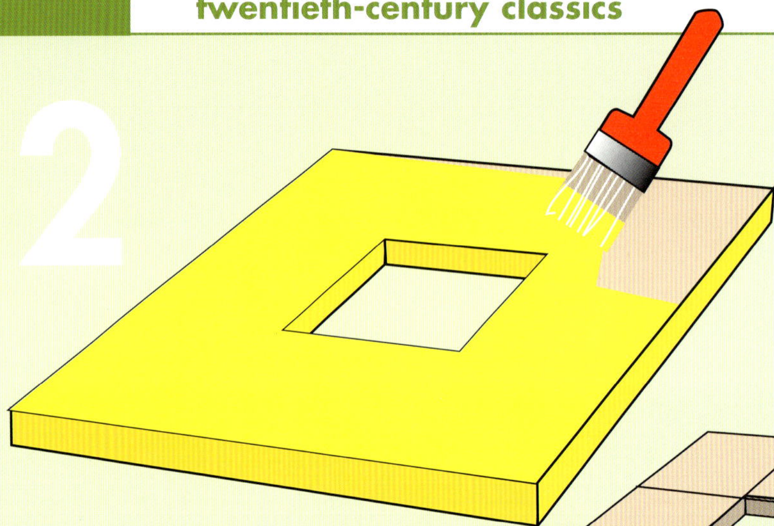

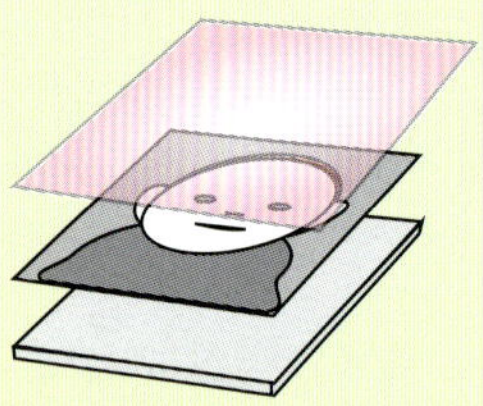

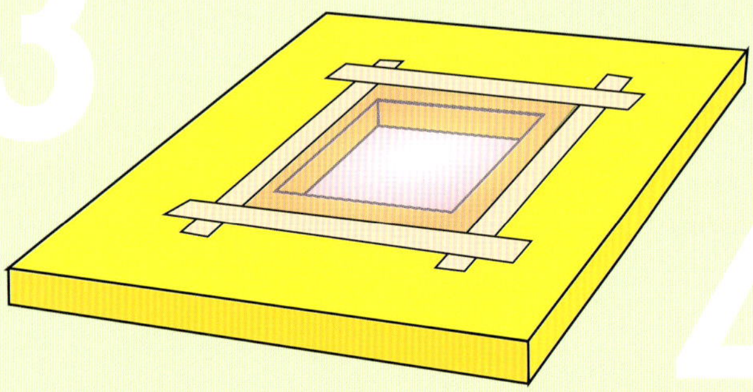

Use a photocopier to enlarge the photograph to 22cm square and cut it out. The contrast should be set at maximum to give the image an authentic screen-print look. Mount the photo onto card using spray adhesive.

Draw a 20cm square in the middle of the MDF by marking off two 20cm intervals on each side and drawing four lines to join them. Cut out the square using a jigsaw, then sand away any rough edges. ❶

Paint the frame with several coats of paint to build up a dense colour. Paint both sides or the MDF will warp. ❷

Stick the acetate centrally to the back of the frame using masking tape ❸, then place the photo behind it and secure in place with more tape. ❹

Fix one screw eye to each side of the back of the frame and twist the picture wire in place between them.

# fifties-style coat rack

**twentieth-century classics**

pages 50–55

**YOU WILL NEED:**

- 40 x 15cm piece of 12mm MDF
- 10mm drill bit
- white paint
- 8 x 1cm lengths of 10mm dowelling
- 8 solid rubber balls in assorted colours
- 2 screws and rawlplugs
- tool kit

1

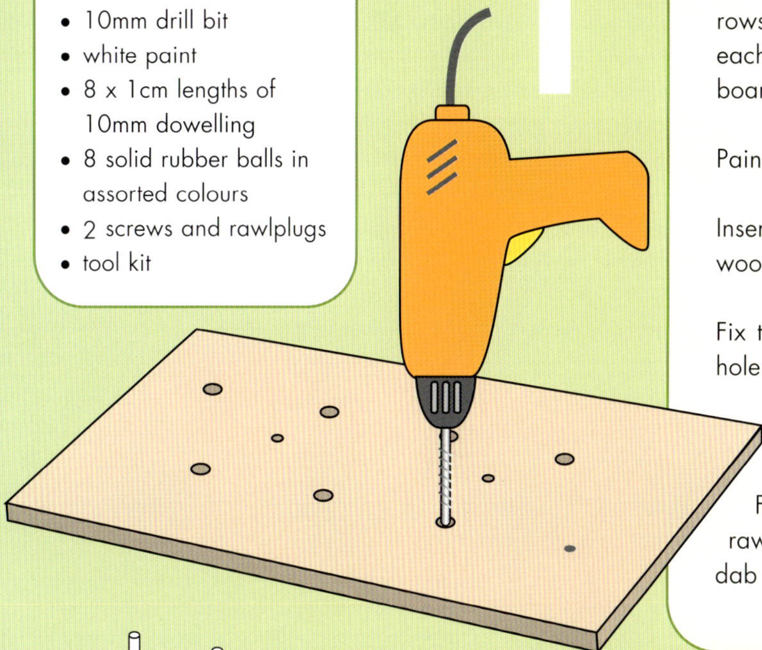

Mark the peg positions on the MDF with two staggered rows of four dots, 10cm apart. Drill a 10mm hole at each dot, then drill two smaller holes in the centre of the board for mounting. ❶ Sand any rough edges.

Paint the board and dowelling white.

Insert a length of dowelling into each hole, securing with wood glue. ❷

Fix the first ball firmly into a clamp and drill a 10mm hole 2cm deep into it. Drop a blob of glue into the hole and fit the ball onto the dowelling. Attach the other balls in the same way, alternating the colours. ❸

Finally, screw the coat rack to the wall using rawlplugs. Disguise the screw heads with filler and a dab of white paint.

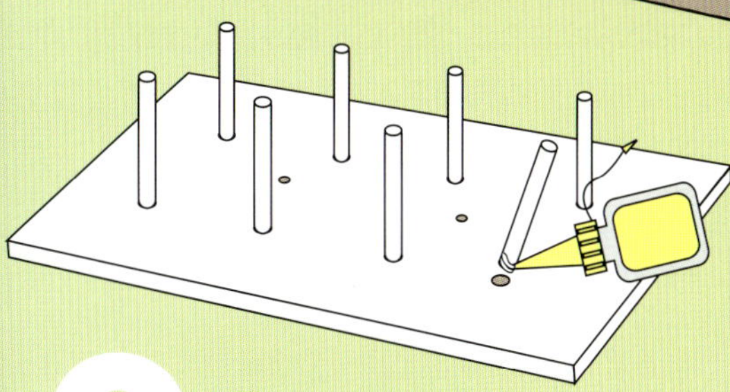

2

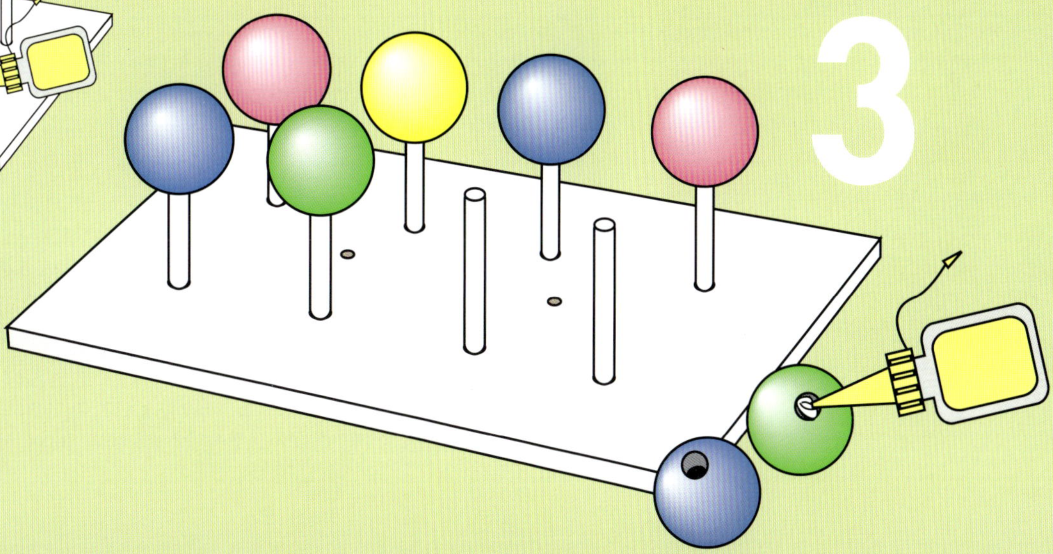

3

pages 56–61

# balloon holdbacks

## disney winnie the pooh

**YOU WILL NEED:**

- 22 x 44cm piece of 8mm MDF
- pair of compasses
- 2 x 20cm lengths of 15mm dowelling
- paint
- 30cm length of 12 x 5cm wood strip
- 15mm drill bit
- 2 x 30cm lengths of piping cord
- screws and rawlplugs
- tool kit

Mark two 20cm circles on the MDF, then draw on the ends of the balloons. Cut out around the outlines and sand any rough edges. ❶

Paint both sides and the edges of the balloons in two different colours. When they are dry add white highlights. ❷

Cut the wood strip into two 10cm and two 5cm lengths and sand them down. Drill a 15mm hole in the centre of each block. Drill two small holes at the edges of the long blocks for mounting on the wall. ❸

Using wood glue, stick a small block to the centre back of each balloon and fix the dowelling into the holes. Glue the mounting blocks to the other ends of the dowelling, making sure they line up with the base of the balloon. ❹

Finish each balloon with a piping cord bow, stitching through to secure. Fix the holdbacks to either side of the window with screws and rawlplugs.

1

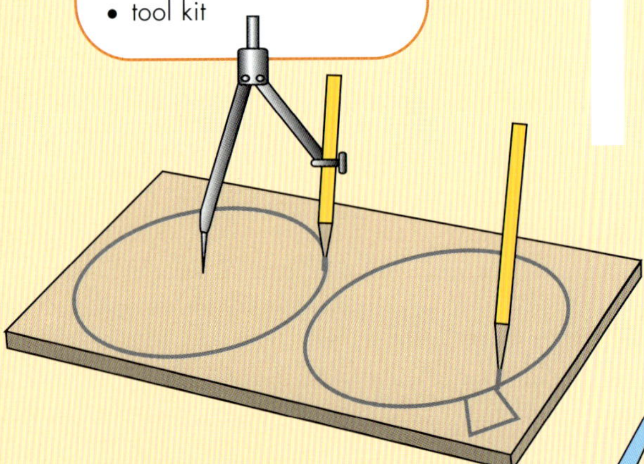

2

3

4

# flower playmat

## disney winnie the pooh

pages 56–61

**YOU WILL NEED:**

- 2 x 1m squares of thick polyester wadding
- 2 x 1m squares of orange cotton fabric
- matching sewing cotton
- 2 x 36cm diameter circles of yellow cotton fabric
- 36cm diameter circle of thin polyester wadding
- non-slip mat backing
- sewing kit

Make a paper pattern for the flower by enlarging the template on page 91 to 96cm diameter, drawing it up on squared paper.

Lay the large pieces of thick wadding out on a flat surface and place the two orange squares on top with their right sides facing. Pin on the pattern and cut out through the four layers, remembering to add an extra 1cm seam allowance all round. ❶

Pin and tack the cotton and wadding together around the outside, then machine stitch 1cm from the edge. Clip small notches into the seam allowance roughly every 5cm and snip between the petals, so the finished flower will lie flat. Be careful not to cut into the stitches.

Cut a 10cm slit in the centre of the flower, through just one layer of cotton. Turn the flower right sides out through this hole. ❷

Make the flower centre in the same way from the yellow cotton and the circle of wadding. ❸

Place the completed centre on to the middle of the flower so the slits are facing each other, then pin and tack it down. Slip stitch in place. ❹

Fix strips of non-slip backing to the mat, so that it will not slide on the floor.

1

2

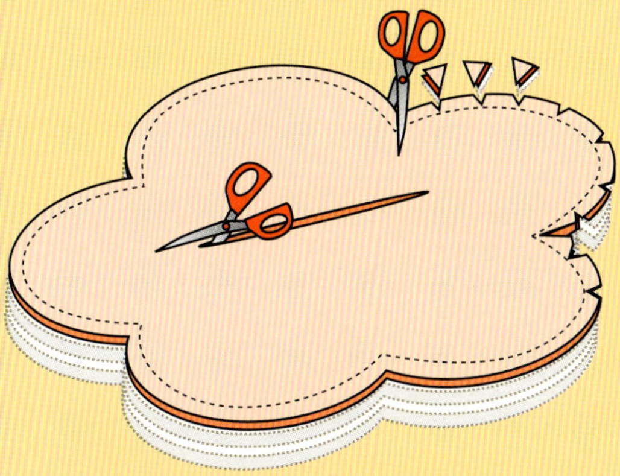

3

4

# bean-bag building blocks

## it's never too early to learn

pages 62–67

**FOR EACH BLOCK YOU WILL NEED:**

- 6 x 15cm squares of fleece fabric
- sewing thread
- polyester toy filling
- sewing kit

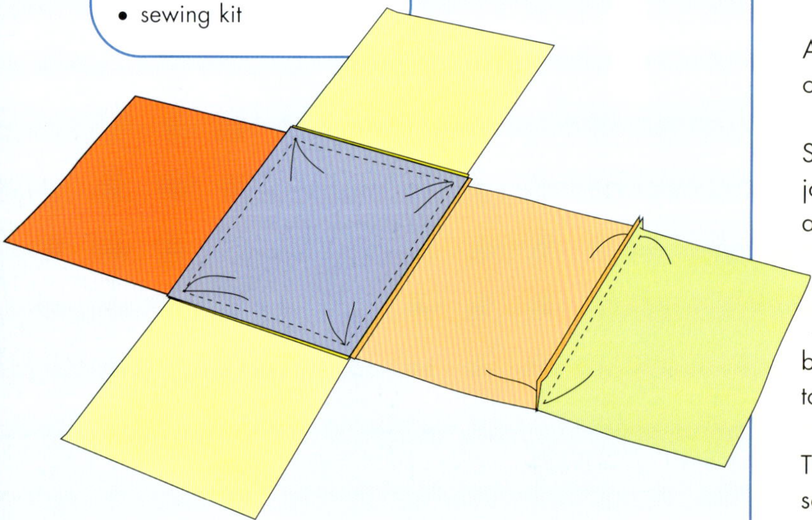

Pin and tack four of the fleece squares together in a row. Machine stitch, using the recommended stitch for jersey fabrics. Leave a seam allowance of 1cm, being sure to start and end each line of stitches 1cm from the edge.

Attach the remaining two squares to the opposite sides of the second square so that you now have a cross. ❶

Sew the arms of the cross together, making a box, then join the two sides of the 'lid'. Tack under the seam allowance on either side of the opening. ❷

Turn the block inside out and ease the corners into shape. Stuff with polyester filling, until the shape is solid but not distorted. Tack and slip stitch the opening securely to complete the cube. ❸

The large block is made in the same way but scaled up so each side is a 50cm square of fleece numbered from one to six. It's filled with a cube of polystyrene beads inside a calico lining. Fit this inside the fleece cover after the side seams have been joined, then slip stitch down the remaining three sides of the lid.

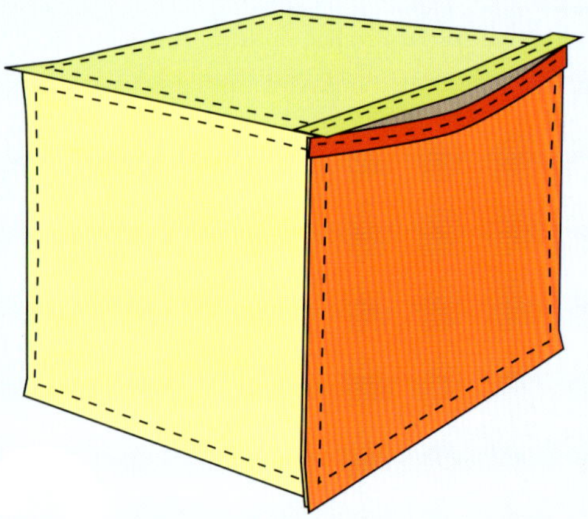

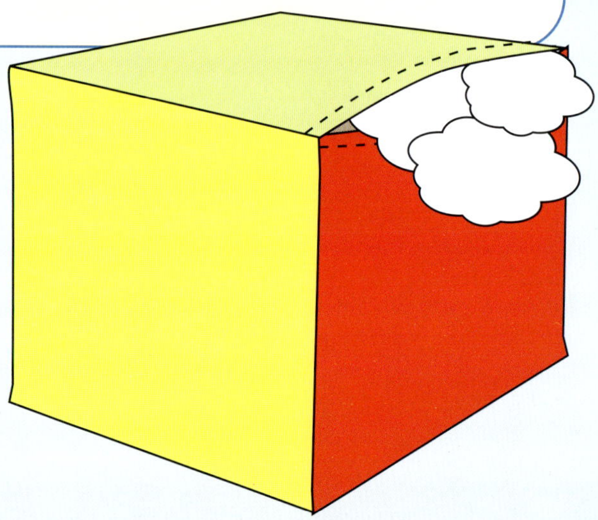

# sheep rug

**down on the farm**

pages 68–73

**YOU WILL NEED:**

- cotton twist bath mat with rubberised backing
- craft felt
- fabric glue
- non-slip mat backing
- sewing kit

1

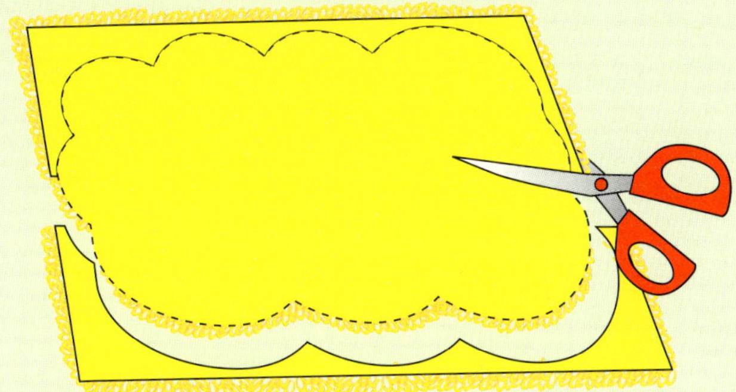

2

3

4

Turn the bath mat wrong side up. Using tailor's chalk, draw a series of curves around the edge to make the shape for the sheep's body. Cut out along the curves. ❶

Enlarge the head and leg of the sheep motif shown here in proportion to the body to make templates for the felt shapes. Trace off the shapes for the face, ear, fleecy hair, leg and hoof, remembering to add an extra 3cm where the shapes will overlap. ❷

Cut out the shapes from different coloured felt. Stick the hooves to the legs with fabric glue, then stick them to the bottom edge of the mat. ❸

Assemble the head adding two felt eyes and a nose, then glue and machine-stitch in place. Using long stab stitches, secure the head firmly to the rug. ❹ Add non-slip backing underneath the felt parts.

As with any rug, our sheep rug should be dry-cleaned.

templates

## doll's house wardrobe

page 77

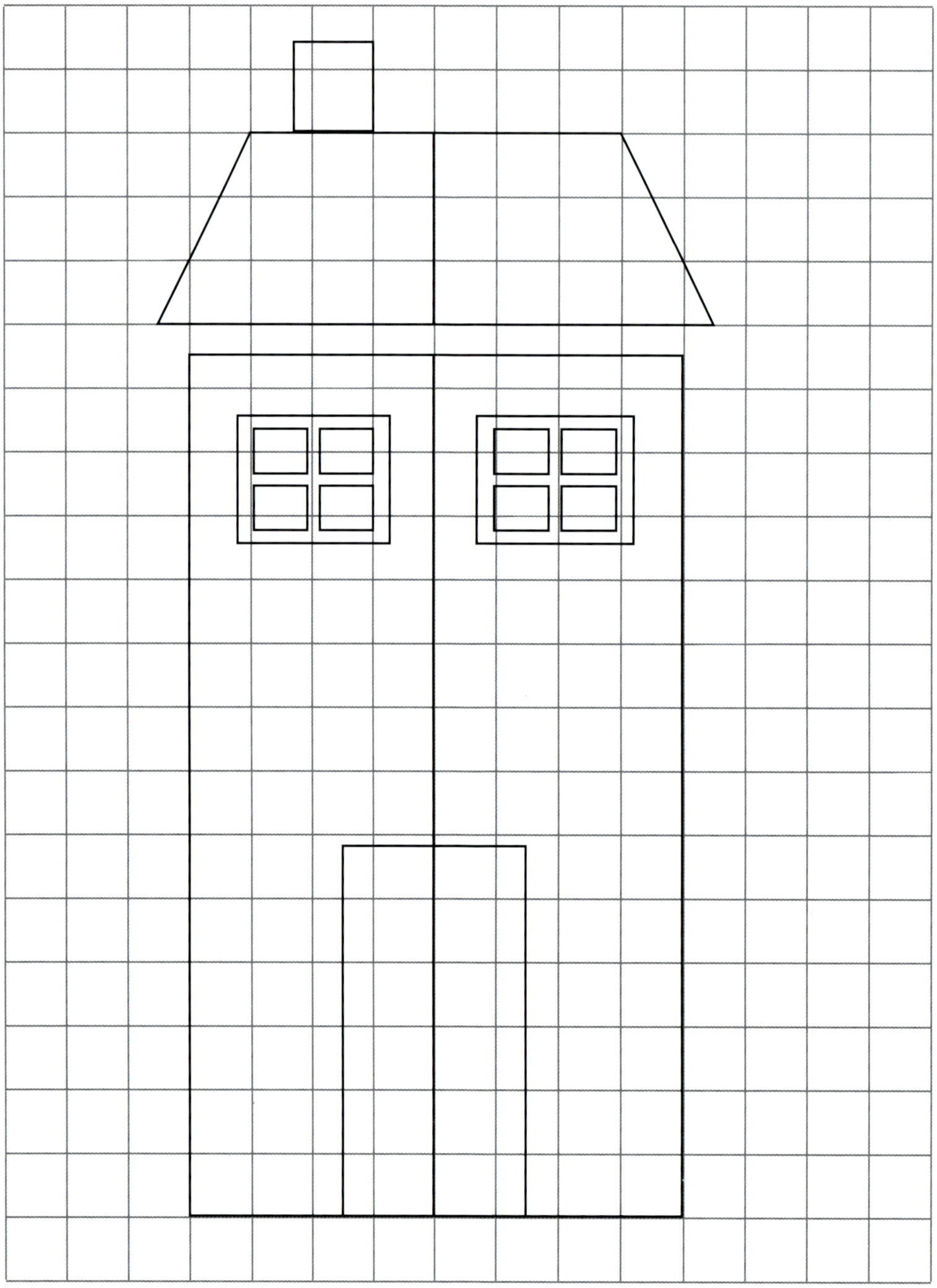

# templates

## flower, mobile, playmat and shelf

pages 77–87

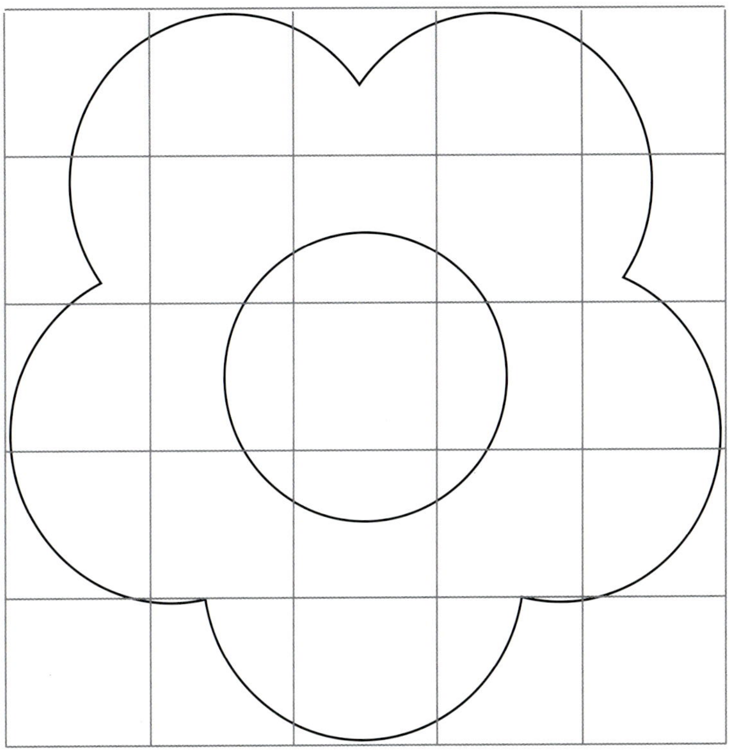

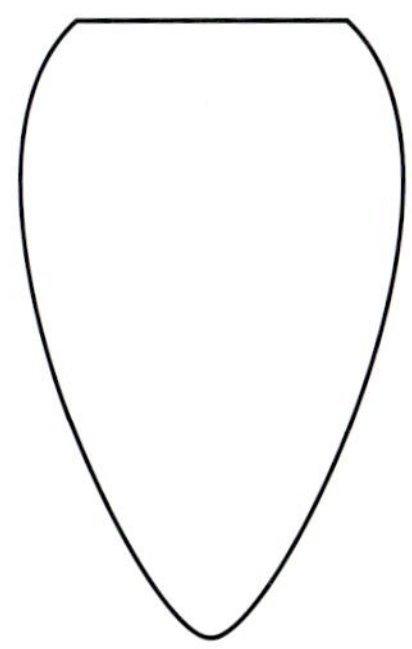

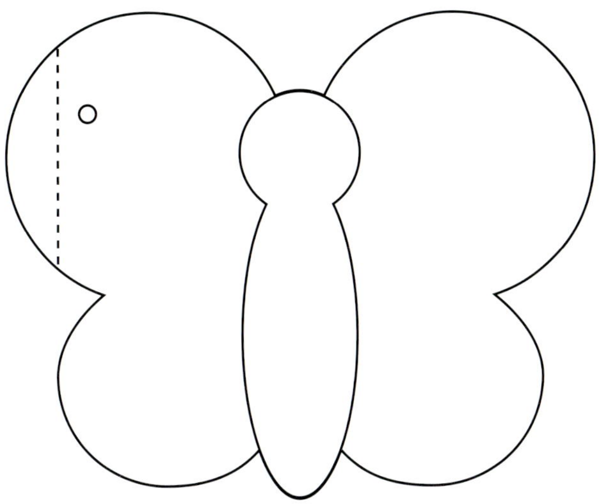

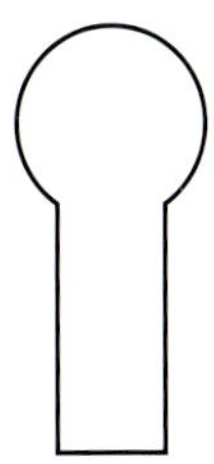

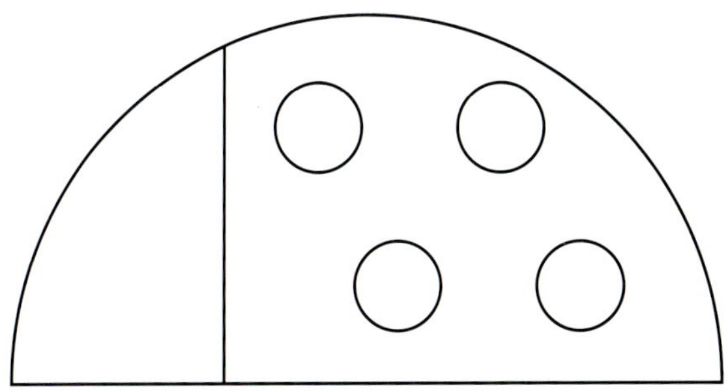

templates

## train toy box

page 80

## cot number plate

page 81

# stockists and suppliers

## B & Q

*for paints – including Benetton Chalkboard Paint – wood, MDF and ironmongery*

B & Q Plc
Portswood House
1 Hampshire Corporate Park
Chandlers Ford
Eastleigh
Hants S053 3YX

**Tel: 023 8025 6256**
*Fax: 023 8025 7480*
**www.diy.com**

## B. BROWN DISPLAY MATERIALS

*for felt*

**Tel: 08705 340340**
**www.bbrown.co.uk**

## DALSOUPLE

*for rubber flooring*

PO Box 140
Bridgwater
Somerset TA5 1HT

**Tel: 01984 667233**
*Fax: 01984 667366*
**www.dalsouple.com**

## HOMEBASE

*for paint, wood, MDF, toy boxes and ironmongery*

Customer Relations Department
Beddington House
Railway Approach
Wallington, SM6 0HB

**Tel: 0870 900 8098**
Fax: 020 8784 7690
**www.homebase.co.uk**

## HOMECRAFT DIRECT

*for craft foam, glue and other craft supplies*

**Tel: 0845 458 4531**
**www.homecraft.co.uk**

## IKEA

*for baskets, desks and office furniture, sofabeds, chairs, non-slip rug backing*

**Tel: 0208 208 5600**
**www.ikea.co.uk**

## JOHN LEWIS PARTNERSHIP

*for non-slip rug backing*

John Lewis Direct
PO Box 369
Exeter EX1 1DH

**Tel: 08456 049 049**
*Fax: 08456 049 050*
**www.johnlewis.com**

## MAKITA INTERNATIONAL EUROPE LTD

*for power tools*

Michigan Drive
Tongwell
Milton Keynes
Bucks MK15 8JD

**Tel: 01908 211678**
*Fax: 01908 211500*

## MOTHERCARE

*for all nursery equipment and furniture*

Department CSC
Cherry Tree Road
Watford
Hertfordshire WD24 6SH

**Tel: 08453 30 40 30**
**www.mothercare.com**

## V. V. ROULEAUX

*for ribbons and trims*

6 Marylebone High Street
London W1M 3PB

**Tel: 020 7224 5179**
*Fax: 020 7224 5193*
**www.vvrouleaux.com**

## WICKES

*for paint, wood, MDF, birch laminate flooring and ironmongery*

Wickes Customer Services
Wickes House
120-138 Station Road
Harrow
Middlesex HA1 2QB

**Tel: 0870 6089001**
*Fax: 020 8863 6225*
**www.wickes.co.uk**

# index

# anna's acknowledgements

Many thanks to Chris King for his great photography and for keeping me supplied with cake, Mike Palmer for being my handyman, and Katie Findlay for holding the whole thing together and for her persistence with the flat bread!

A special thanks to Jane Lawton of Mothercare and her fantastic team, Sharon Kralj for her sewing and Vikki Collar for her dancing, and to Lucinda Ganderton for her wonderful way with my words.

And last but not least, thanks to Makita (UK) Ltd for the loan of the power tools, Dalsouple for the rubber flooring, Homecraft Direct for the craft materials, and Linked Resourcing, The Design Company and Zorbit Babycare for help with the propping.

**picture credits** **1–4** Chris King; **6** Mothercare; **8** IPC Syndication/© Homes & Ideas/Niall McDiarmid; **9** Retna/Sandra Lousada; **10** Gettyimages/Tosca Radigonda; **12 above:** Sanoma Syndication/John Dummer; **12 below:** Sanoma Syndication/Dolf Straatemeier; **13** Red Cover/Verity Welstead; **14 left:** IPC Syndication/© Homes &Ideas/Trevor Richards; **14 right:** Mothercare; **15** Sanoma Syndication/Carel Verduin; **20 above:** Gettyimages/Denis Boissavy; **20 below:** Sanoma Syndication/Carel Verduin; **21–22** Mothercare; **23** Sanoma Syndication/John Dummer; **24 above:** IPC Syndication/© Homes & Ideas/Bill Reavell; **24 centre:** Camera Press/Woman's Value; **24 below:** IPC Syndication/© Homes & Ideas/Simon Whitmore; **25** Sanoma Syndication/John Dummer; **26 above:** Retna/Sandra Lousada; **26 below:** Gettyimages/Andy Cox; **27** Gettyimages/Steve Casimiro.